THE
PERSONAL
MANAGEMENT
HANDBOOK

THE PERSONAL MANAGEMENT HANDBOOK

How to make the most of your potential

Consultant Editor
JOHN MULLIGAN
Human Potential Resource Group
University of Surrey

Sphere Reference

A Marshall Edition
Conceived, edited and designed by
Marshall Editions Ltd
170 Piccadilly
London W1V 9DD

Editor
Ricki Ostrov

Art Editor
Roger Kohn

Design Assistants
Vanilla Beer
Sarah Lloyd

Managing Editor
Ruth Binney

Production
Barry Baker
Janice Storr

Illustrators
János Márffy
Graham Rosewarne

Indexer
Kathie Gill

First published 1988 by
Sphere Books Ltd
27 Wrights Lane
London W8 5TZ
Copyright © 1988
Marshall Editions Ltd

TRADE
MARK

SPHERE

Filmset in Century Old Style by Servis Filmsetting
Limited, Manchester, UK.
Origination in Hong Kong by Regent Publishing
Services Ltd.
Printed and bound by Usines Brepols SA, Belgium.

1   2   3   4   5   92   91   90   89   88

John Mulligan, MA, DipEd is the director of the Human Potential Resource Group. He is an adult educator committed to adapting and developing psychotherapeutic and sociological discoveries as practical means of living and learning, to developing people's individual and collective potential, and to promoting holistic forms of professional practice. He acts as a counsellor at the Devonshire Clinic, a multi-disciplinary health care practice in central London.

CONTRIBUTORS

Elizabeth Adeline is a psychological educator and practitioner of humanistic psychology who works with groups, couples and individuals. She is a member of Redwood Women's Training Association, the Institute for the Development of Human Potential, and of the management team of 'Openings', a centre for personal growth, change and healing in Bath.

Robert Adlam, BSc Psych is academic director of the accelerated promotion programme for police officers with outstanding management potential at the Police Staff College, Bramshill, Hampshire. He specializes in holistic management development.

Maurice Bailey works in management and consultancy for a major oil company.

Meg Bond, SRN is assistant director of the Human Potential Resource Group and the author of several books on stress and assertiveness. She is a humanistic educator with a background in nursing and nurse education.

Michael Eales, MA is a freelance facilitator. He is founder and codirector of Praxis and facilitates many training groups, including a programme at the University of Surrey. He is currently making a documentary for Channel 4.

Anouk Grave, MIDHP is codirector of Praxis. She specializes in the design and facilitation of training programmes for trainers and practitioners in education, industry and the professions.

Marie-Louise Hayward, MSc, SRN is a director of MLM Consultants, specialists in management development. She also acts as a consultant to industry, commerce, the health service, Brunel University and Henley Management College.

Kate Hopkinson, BS Psych is a management consultant with the Coverdale Organisation and a consultant in humanistic psychology. She specializes in team-building, organizational change and developing stress-management policies with individuals and organizations. She also practises as a psychotherapist with individuals and couples.

CONTENTS

THE HUMAN POTENTIAL RESOURCE GROUP

The Human Potential Resource Group is a human resources development unit within the Department of Educational Studies at the University of Surrey, Guildford, England. Formerly the Human Potential Research Project, it is the longest established centre for humanistic and transpersonal education in Europe.

The project offers a wide range of personal, professional and organizational development opportunities to the industrial and commercial sector, to public services and to individuals who wish to develop their personal and/or professional effectiveness.

The aims of the project are:
● To provide practical resources for the research and development of human capacities and potential.
● To promote values and educational practice which empower individuals and encourage creative interdependence between people in social and organizational settings.
● To encourage rounded or holistic development of the person and the integration of personal and professional development.

The personal effectiveness programme includes short courses which provide:
● A wide range of methods for personal development and self-management.
● An opportunity to explore human capacities which are often not addressed in mainstream education.

● A balance to traditional personal and professional development by emphasizing internal well-being and linking the social, mental, physical, spiritual and emotional dimensions of living and learning.
● A variety of methods which promote more productive and satisfying relationships in diverse settings.

The professional development programme offers courses covering:
● A wide range of methods for enhancing the participant's capacity to learn from experience.
● Interpersonal and counselling skills training for professionals.
● Training for practitioners, educators and trainers in holistic methods of individual and group facilitation.
● Practical methods for the design and management of in-service education and training programmes.

The project also provides in-service staff training and organizational development programmes ranging from one day courses to long-term programmes spanning years. It has at its disposal the facilitation and consultancy skills of the project staff and an international network of associate facilitators. Some of these facilitators work in the industrial sector and others work as consultants in both public and private sectors. In addition, the project draws upon the computer and distance learning expertise, audio-visual material and other resources available within the University.

INTRODUCTION

In today's complex world, just surviving requires skilful personal management. Realizing your own potential, and helping to realize that of others, demands highly sensitive and well-developed personal management skills. Rounded development, including the ability to manage yourself and others, is now being formally recognized as a vital part of the manager's toolkit. And effective personal management is essential if you are to make the most of your life and your potential, whether you are managing a large organization, your own life affairs, or bringing up a family.

The Personal Management Handbook helps you take charge of your life and increase the effectiveness of your relationships with others, both within the sphere of your working life and outside it. By drawing together a wide range of information, and through its many practical self-help suggestions, it will make you more aware of yourself and your unique potential, and show you that you have the capacity for realizing that potential to the full.

This handbook is about success in your work and your relationships, but it goes a step beyond mere achievement. Many people who have reached the pinnacle of a career often find themselves asking 'Is this all there is?'. On offer in these pages is a means of effectively managing many challenges, but within the context of a meaningful vision of your own individual purpose or pathway in life. By placing self-management in a 'whole life' setting, the book shows you how to manage your internal world of feeling, imagination, thought and will, as well as the external world of relationships, career and social groups.

The theory and practical advice offered are derived from the authors' many years of experience in helping people to improve the way they function and to increase their level of personal satisfaction. You will probably find this most useful at times when your life experiences make you aware of particular needs. You may, for example, feel a need to improve your communication skills, deal better with difficult people, or develop your career. Once you are aware of such needs, the book will guide you to an increased understanding of what may be happening to you, raise your awareness of the options that are open, and pinpoint the skills that will improve both your self-management and your relationships with others.

The book begins by showing you how to map out your life – as you are aware of it now and as you would like it to be. The journey format of these life maps will help you illuminate the dynamic and developmental nature of your existence. Thus you start by mapping where you have come from and end by mapping where you are going. Through these maps you will get to know the 'territory' of your life in a way that gives you a greater sense of your potential and your direction.

Having mapped your life, you can then use the rest of the book to deepen your awareness and develop the skills required for your onward journey. The methods described here are tried and tested. Test them for yourself by carrying out the suggested exercises, and by practising and reviewing your skills and strategies. Ideally, share this work with a partner – a friend or close colleague – or with a supportive group.

Once you have read and used this book, you may feel that you need more. If so, you might find a workshop a good place to start, or a professional counsellor might prove a useful resource. The Human Potential Resource Group at the University of Surrey, Guildford, has been promoting personal effectiveness and self-management for many years. This book is a distillation of what the facilitators of workshops at the project – who are the authors of the book – have found most worthwhile. We hope the ideas work for you.

MANAGING YOU

Life maps are tools for self-discovery, and guides to various aspects of your life as you experience it. They are a way of outlining the territory, signposting the terrain and becoming familiar with the landscape of your life.

Maps can help you connect up the various aspects of your life by establishing links between your past, present and future, and the different levels of your being, for example, your mind, body, emotions and spirit. They can help you focus in on the detail of specific areas of your life.

All maps can help you become more aware of yourself, including your strengths and weaknesses, and enable you to plot any changes you might wish to make.

To make best use of maps you will need to consider a mapping system which connects all the types of map described in this book to the central thread of your life.

This system has been adapted from one developed by consultant John Heron. It stretches backward into your past and forward into your future, linking historical facts of your life to date with the potential that may be realized in the future.

YOUR LIFE MAP

This map can be used to explore your life as a whole or a specific aspect or concern you may have. It is progressive and sequenced as follows.

Your life's journey
- Who am I?
- Where have I come from?
- Where am I going?
- What is stopping me?
- How will I get there?
- What help do I need?
- What will it be like when I get there?

Each of the following sections will address successive aspects of this map. 'Who am I?' is concerned with your identity. It pinpoints the various aspects of your life and the way your energy is devoted.

'Where have I come from?' seeks to outline your personal history, or the historical antecedents to the aspects of your life you happen to be exploring.

'Where am I going?' attempts to amplify your potential, illuminate your direction and destination in life,

define your goals and establish your guiding vision.

'What is stopping me?' looks at the constraints, the blocks and the obstacles which may prevent or hinder your progress toward your goals.

'How will I get there?' tries to establish the steps that you will need to take to reach your goal. It is a specific plan which outlines the logistics of your journey.

'What help do I need?' deals with the resources and support you will need on your journey. It

states the skills you need to develop, the qualities required and the people who will assist you.

'What will it be like when I get there?' is an imaginative construction of what life will be like at your journey's end. It helps you identify in detail with the imaginative vision of where you want to get to. It evokes the emotional, sensational and desirable. In this way it mobilizes your energy and motivation in preparation for action.

★ TRY THIS NOW!

Get seven sheets of paper and coloured pencils. Sit quietly in a relaxed position. Breathe deeply several times, allowing any physical or mental tension to flow away with each out breath.

In turn, meditate on each of the seven stages of the map. Notice any words, images, feelings or thoughts which emerge as you focus on each question.

Spend five minutes on each question. Then write or draw what you have noticed. If you cannot do it all concentrate on the most significant aspects. Continue until all seven are done.

What have you discovered about yourself? Would you like to know more? If so, each of your sheets can be further amplified by the suggestions on the following pages. The result should clarify your awareness of yourself and your direction in life.

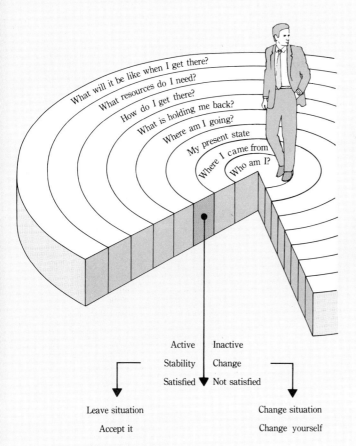

What will it be like when I get there?
What resources do I need?
How do I get there?
What is holding me back?
Where am I going?
My present state
Where I came from
Who am I?

Active	Inactive
Stability	Change
Satisfied	Not satisfied

Leave situation

Accept it

Change situation

Change yourself

When examining your present state you will need to look at how satisfied you are with various areas of your life. This will involve determining how active you are in different areas and whether you are happy with the situation or seek a change. See Mapping Your Development (pp. 18–19) for more information about how to determine this.

When you are asked the question 'Who are you?' you will probably respond by giving your name, which is your identity tag. If asked the question again you may give a deeper answer which refers to your nationality, social position, work or achievements.

All of these refer to external sources of identity. Asking the question yet again may even make you focus on your inner sources of identity such as beliefs, values, interests, worries or ambitions in life. The questions can be continually asked until all the answers have been exhausted and you are left with a wordless experience of your own being.

That is probably the nearest you can get to the answer. This encounter with who you really are – stripped of all your appendages – is often a powerful experience, though one that is difficult to articulate and communicate.

Different people express their identity in different ways. Some express it through their clothes or their possessions, others through their job or the car they drive. Most people seem to gain their identity through reference points outside themselves. Fewer people seem to gain their identity from internal sources within themselves.

It is knowledge of these internal sources of your identity that relate to self-awareness and self-conscious. Other internal sources relate to your self-image, your beliefs, values, desires and needs.

BRANCH PATTERNS

One useful way of mapping out what you consciously know about yourself, both your internal and your social identity, is to draw a branch pattern which connects possible answers to the central questions.

Each answer may then be further amplified into smaller, connected branches which indicate subdivisions. This method can be used to brainstorm and develop awareness of and interconnections between various aspects of your life.

Guided imagery
A second way of discovering who you are is to experience a guided visualization which helps you get to know your internal community or your subpersonalities. These are internal roles or parts of you which emerge both at work and play. They include, for example, the critic, the dreamer, the bully, the nurturer, the child and the parent.

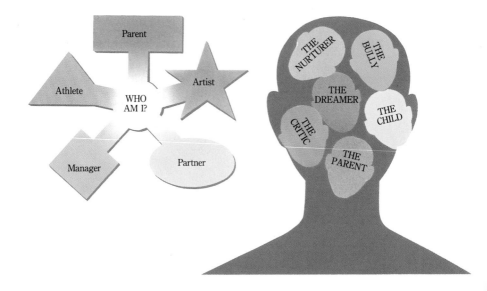

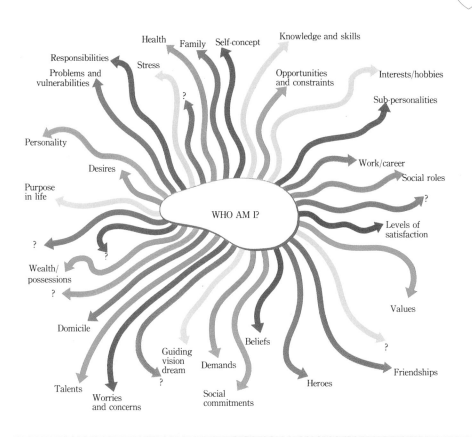

Health Family Self-concept Knowledge and skills

Responsibilities
Stress
Problems and
vulnerabilities

Opportunities
and constraints

Interests/hobbies

Sub-personalities

?

Personality

Desires

Work/career

Social roles

Purpose
in life

WHO AM I?

?

?

Levels of
satisfaction

?

Wealth/
possessions

?

Values

Domicile

Beliefs

?

Guiding
vision
dream
?

Demands

Friendships

Talents

Heroes

Worries
and concerns

Social
commitments

★ TEST YOURSELF!

To get to know your internal community, imagine you leave your front door in the morning. You walk along your usual path, then you notice a new path leading away to the left. You follow this path which takes you through sunlit countryside with its sounds, colours, smells and landscape.

Your path leads you into a forest which gradually darkens to twilight as you go deeper into it.

In the distance you can see a sunlit clearing with a house at its centre. As you approach the house you notice a sign on the door and you read what it says. You enter the house and spend some time exploring the house and meeting the residents.

Notice in detail what happens. When you have explored the house you go outside again and face the house. The door opens and out come

the residents. You are approached by each one in turn. Notice what takes place and how you feel.

When you have met all of them you slowly return through the forest to the path. Take some time to gather your thoughts and feelings and reflect on what you discovered.

Take some time, also, to write about or draw your findings. It is useful to assume that the house is a symbol of your self

and its inhabitants are your internal community.

How did you get on with them? What did they have to say? Were they familiar? What was the atmosphere in the house like? Were there many rooms, floors or any unusual features? What does all of this tell you about yourself and your relationship with your internal community? Is there anything you would like to change?

Getting to know yourself means being familiar with your history, that is with all that has happened in your life up to now. Mapping out the major events, achievements, choices and influences on your life will give you some idea of how you came to be the unique person you are today.

MAPPING YOUR ROOTS

Mapping your background should help you realize that what you are is not just a matter of chance. You were formed by means of a variety of influences and as you grow you can be a major formative influence in your own life. This map should help you understand your legacy from the past, including your strengths and handicaps, joys and sorrows.

It is important when doing this that you do not do it with the attitude of avoiding responsibility or blaming your fortune or misfortune on others. Instead it will help you to illuminate the present through reflection on the past and enable you to take more charge of your future.

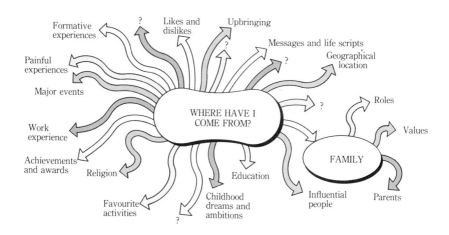

★ TEST YOURSELF!

Take a piece of paper and draw a line from one side of the page to the other. This horizontal line represents the passage of time from the beginning of your existence until the end of your life. The vertical dimension represents your feelings of physical and mental well-being. Place the positive feelings above the line and the negative ones below it.

Map out the significant events and times in your life chronologically and according to how they related to your state of well-being.

Notice changes in well-being, how they came about and what beliefs or attitudes you formed in response to them. Are they still useful or do they need changing?

You may wish to share these observations with a friend to clarify them further and make them more alive. Self-disclosure, or talking about yourself to an accepting listener, is one of the best ways of getting to know yourself. Their observations and feedback may also be valuable and the experience of sharing at this level will undoubtedly deepen your friendship.

DISCOVERING YOUR ROOTS

Understanding your background will throw into relief the decisions and choices you have made.

Mapping the formative influences and identifying the underlying or connecting themes in your life experience may help you discover what is truly you, as distinct from what others might have wanted you to be.

Becoming an autonomous individual means separating yourself out from this background and finding your own identity. This background may be comfortable, and you may be reluctant to separate yourself from it. Alternatively you may feel unsupported or smothered by your background. Lovingly separating yourself is necessary to find your true self.

YOUR LIFE SCRIPTS

Although it may seem to you that you had little control or influence in your early years you did make certain choices. These decisions may have been useful at an earlier age but may now be a hindrance.

Get to know these early decisions and the accompanying attitudes and beliefs. This will help you to be more in charge of your current behaviour.

These decisions, sometimes called life scripts or constructs, can remain at the periphery of your consciousness until you look for them. They can have an empowering (power providing) or a crippling effect, as well as all the levels in between. Your life scripts may need to be re-evaluated and replaced by more constructive scripts if you are to achieve your goals.

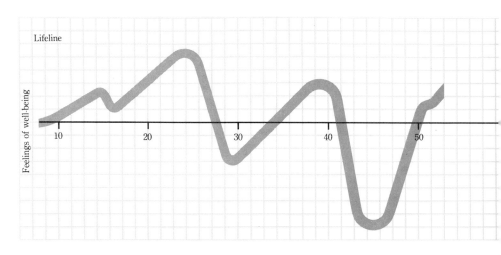

Lifeline

Feelings of well-being

10   20   30   40   50

★ TRY THIS NOW!

Set up a branch pattern around the question 'Where have I come from?' Let your associations build the pattern connecting events and decisions as appropriate.

Taking various events or experiences in turn, try to evoke the sensory feelings and details of the experience as if it were happening right now. This will improve your memory of the event. Take your time and allow yourself to dialogue internally and express your feeling toward the protagonists.

Listen to their response. Notice what decisions you took at that time, whether these still operate in your current life and whether they help or hinder you.

You may find it useful to do this exercise with a friend. The more you put into this exercise in terms of reflection and coverage of events in your life the more you will get from it.

The aim is to try to clear up any unfinished business you may have in your past life and close it so that your attention will be free for your intentions and your life's journey.

Once you have identified who you are on your current journey you will need to clarify where you are going. Many people set off in all directions at once or feel that their energies are split in so many different ways that progress becomes difficult.

Only by finding a direction that honours and resolves the conflicts, desires or external pressures can you create a synthesis or combination which allows progress. It is important for everyone to find the underlying theme of their guiding vision.

MAKING CHOICES

Every choice that you make probably means discarding many others. You may be anxious about choosing one way or the other when you reach major crossroads in your life because you want to keep all your options open. But the result is that you end up in a state of paralysis and with a lack of progress.

People have many crossroads in their lives, and these include life stages and transitions (see pp. 74–75). They are a time for clarifying your values, reconnecting with your guiding images, your life and career plans.

Once you set your priorities or decide where you are going, and ensure that it is consistent with who you are, it will be less difficult to discard available options. A fear of letting go of your options may well mean that you do not know where you are going.

Knowing where you are going requires that you know where you are now, that is, you must know what your point of embarkation is. Clarifying the present state of your affairs will at least help you be aware of the direction in which you are presently headed. You may find that it may not be where you think you are headed, or even where you want to be going.

MAPPING YOUR DEVELOPMENT

To map out your development draw a grid on a large sheet of paper. List the various areas of your life down one side of the page and head the columns as shown.

For each area of your life, write how you are active in that area. Also list whether you are happy with that state of affairs. Then expand on your answer.

Finally, identify what change you desire if any. You may group areas of your life together and invent headings for whatever areas are appropriate to your own life.

It is essential also that you try to be as comprehensive as possible in your coverage, since this may uncover stagnant areas or new possibilities in your life.

		Health	Education
Active			
Inactive			
Satisfied			
Dissatisfied			
Change desired			

★ TEST YOURSELF!

A useful way of prioritizing is by imagining you had a year to live. How would you spend your time and energy? Imagine doing these things you have chosen. How does it feel?

Now you have six months to live, then just a week. Notice how your priorities, and feelings about them, change as you imagine yourself living then. What have you learned about your priorities and your values? Can you bring this to bear on your choice in decision making?

MAPPING ENERGY EXPENDITURE

To map your energy expenditure, draw a pie chart and try to indicate as accurately as possible how you distribute your time over the various areas of your life. This will give you some sense of the areas which sap your energy and which ones energize you.

When you have finished that chart,

draw another one which shows how you would like your time to be distributed. This should help you emphasize the need for checking your energy against your priorities. It will also indicate that you need to cut down in one area if you are to expand in another.

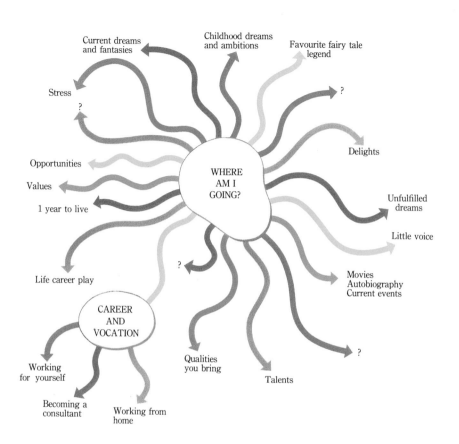

Current dreams and fantasies

Childhood dreams and ambitions

Favourite fairy tale legend

Stress

?

Opportunities

Values

1 year to live

WHERE AM I GOING?

Delights

Unfulfilled dreams

Little voice

Life career play

CAREER AND VOCATION

?

Movies
Autobiography
Current events

?

Working for yourself

Qualities you bring

Talents

Becoming a consultant

Working from home

★ TRY THIS NOW!

Create a branch pattern in response to the question 'Where am I going?' noting all those factors which indicate a calling, a vocation or an inspiration. These may include emerging opportunities, childhood symbols,

dreams, fairy tales or biographies of great people. Also list those factors which delight and energize you.

Relate your pattern with the other work you have carried out so far in mapping your life and see if any theme or

direction emerges.

Whether you find a direction or whether you have to explore each option in turn you will need to:
● *Evaluate the option.*
● *Deliberate the pros and cons.*
● *Identify its implications.*

● *Check your level of motivation in relation to accomplishing it.*

If you find a number of directions you will need to see how they relate to one another. You may have to prioritize them and discard some, at least for now.

Making individual choices invariably entails running into obstacles and having to work within constraints in the process of moving toward your goals. They may be a legacy from your past or an indication of the difficulty of the terrain of your journey. The blocks may be clear and conscious, vague or unconscious.

By raising these blocks to conscious awareness you can choose a way of dealing with them. Some people use brute force, some use cunning, some get around them while others avoid them. Your ability to surmount such difficulties can be a measure of your motivation, your skills, and whether or not you are on your true path.

Some people find it easy to recognize what is or might be blocking their progress, others do not. Some think they know but do not, yet others know but do not realize it. Still others have a vague idea but cannot clarify it so that it becomes useful.

EXPLORING THE BLOCKAGE

Making branch patterns and formulating what is stopping you in the form of a problem works well when you have some degree of awareness or can articulate a problem. Often, however, you may not be able to do this.

You may feel stuck or have a vague sense of blockage which you have not yet found a way to articulate and bring to conscious awareness. The exercise opposite may help you to identify and become more aware of what is stopping you moving on.

Problem statement

Monitor and adapt

Outline effects

Implement

Identify causes

Choice of solution

Brainstorming solutions

State criteria for effective solution

★ TRY THIS NOW!

The simplest way of identifying your blocks and constraints is to brainstorm by listing those to which you can gain access at a conscious level. Drawing a branch pattern can help you to see relationships between various blocks to your progress.

It is important to be as specific as possible. Then, if you can formulate the block in terms of a problem, you will be able to make use of a problem solving cycle for identifying a solution to it (see Managing Yourself Effectively pp. 78–79).

Difficulties likely to be encountered from a personal point of view will bear significant similarity to difficulties you have encountered previously. You may or may not be aware of what caused these difficulties or how you may have created them through your own beliefs and behaviour.

★ TEST YOURSELF!

Sit on a cushion facing a wall. Imagine this wall is your blockage (close your eyes if this helps you). See if you can form an image of your blockage in your mind.

What does it look like? For example, imagine its colour, shape, size, and texture. Allow yourself time to notice all you can about it. Is it a person, an object, an idea? Notice your thoughts, feelings and attitudes as you sit facing this blockage.

Now become the block, sitting with your back against the wall and facing the cushion. See if you can sense what it is like being this blockage. How do you feel and think? What is your attitude toward the person who has been sitting on the cushion? Do you like or dislike this person? As the blockage, say what your purpose in life is.

Once you have taken time to explore the blockage from the inside, as it were,

begin to speak to yourself (the empty cushion). What does the blockage need to say? Is it telling you to slow down, not to go in this particular direction?

Allow the blockage to communicate as much as possible. Then become yourself and try shifting back to the cushion and responding to the blockage from there. Continue the dialogue by speaking in turn from each position. Let each have its say, sharing demands,

resentments and appreciations. See if they can negotiate a way of meeting the needs of both positions and relieving the blockage.

If the blockage is an internal one you may also find it useful if you get the blockage to dialogue with significant others in your life, such as your partner or children. The results can be surprising and may well illuminate a blockage and create a way to resolve it.

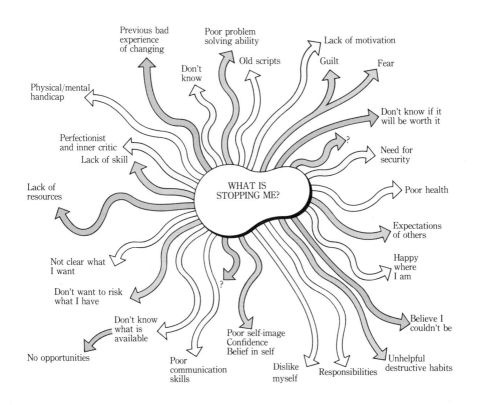

Many good decisions have never come to fruition for want of an effective plan. Some people have an idea and go straight into action only to find that the task of realizing their intention was greater than they had expected. They may find that they have neither time, energy or motivation for their decision. The antidote to this problem is careful planning.

First, you need to identify how you are going to get from where you are now to where you have decided you want to be. Second, this plan may need to be broken down into practical stages or steps. Third, these steps will need to be organized into the sequence in which they can be carried out, stating the specific timing of the action required. You will then need to identify what resources and help you need to progress toward a successful conclusion.

FORCE FIELD ANALYSIS

This method of mapping how to get to where you want to be, developed by social scientist Kurt Lewin, assumes that you are in a state of equilibrium, however stable. This is held in place by forces pushing in opposing directions for and against.

Force field analysis helps you map the forces for and against the change you want to make by representing your present position as a horizontal line which is converged upon by lines representing opposing forces. The length of the vertical line signifies the relative strength of the force.

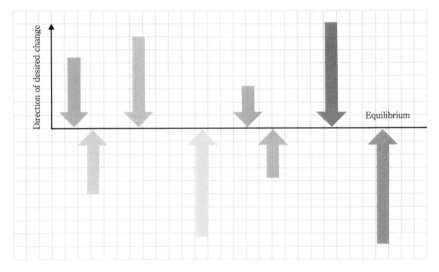

The options available to you to move in the direction of the required change are to:
- Increase the forces for the change.
- Decrease the forces against the change.
- Do both simultaneously.
- Introduce new forces for the change.
- Reduce the forces for the change. Your own pressure for may be causing the reaction against.

★ TRY THIS NOW!

Draw a branch pattern that associates to the question 'How will I get there?'. Identify all the possible steps that might help you progress toward your goal, however fantastic or unrealistic it may seem. You can be practical later.

Often some of these outrageous, humorous or illogical suggestions may hold the key concept for the most effective solution. You can then evaluate these options according to your own values, the available information, the constraints and their practicality to decide which are the most promising solutions to the problem. You may well find that your final choice includes a range of solutions or aspects synthesized from different possible solutions.

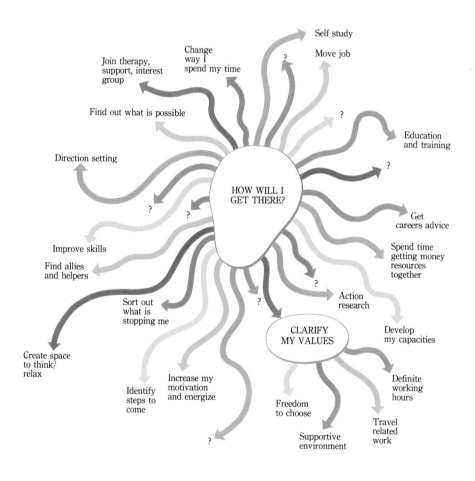

Self study

Move job

Change way I spend my time

?

Join therapy, support, interest group

Find out what is possible

?

Education and training

Direction setting

?

HOW WILL I GET THERE?

?

?

Get careers advice

Improve skills

Find allies and helpers

Spend time getting money resources together

Sort out what is stopping me

?

?

Action research

Create space to think/ relax

CLARIFY MY VALUES

Develop my capacities

Identify steps to come

Increase my motivation and energize

Freedom to choose

Definite working hours

Supportive environment

Travel related work

?

Whenever you take on a new task or project, you will need to have the correct resources available and at hand. Finding yourself lacking in the resources you need may prove disastrous. It may mean you have to call the whole project off, but at the very least it will result in frustrating delays.

Therefore you will need to map out what resources you will need and when you will need them, what resources you have to acquire before you start, and which you can pick up along the way. You might consider resources under the following headings:
- Personal
- People
- Materials

PERSONAL RESOURCES

The personal resources you presently possess can be identified by engaging in some form of assessment. This can range from self-assessment and gaining feedback from friends and colleagues to more formal psychological and educational testing.

The assessment will need to address a number of areas, including your qualities, knowledge, skills, attitudes and beliefs, and will depend on the change you are seeking.

You will then need to compare your personal resources with those that will be necessary if you are to reach your goal and maintain yourself satisfactorily when you get there.

This comparison will help you identify those resources you will need to develop before you begin, or those you will need along the way. (See also Developing Your Capabilities pp. 50–65.)

PEOPLE AS RESOURCES

Making sure you have the resources to support you, especially people, is absolutely essential if you want to give yourself a decent chance of succeeding.

At work you may find an older, experienced member of staff you admire who will act as a mentor and guide. You may find work colleagues are willing to give you feedback, or you may find a friend who will listen to you and constructively question your ideas and progress.

At home, you may need to engage the cooperation and support of your family, especially if you are undertaking a major project which also has implications for them. It may be that they will see less of you and have to carry a greater share of everyday chores for a period. They may even be actively engaged in your journey.

Besides work and home, there are also many possibilities for finding people who can be sources of information and help. You can join ongoing support groups or join or build networks of like-minded people. You can attend one of the many self-development workshops, or one of the counselling or therapy sessions now available.

Make sure you work with people who really have your interests at heart, that they do not interfere in ways you do not want, and that they do not take over.

Also make sure they have some empathy and affection for you, and that they are also willing to confront you supportively when necessary. Sometimes you will need to put up with some person you do not like to learn what is of value to you. (See also Support Systems pp. 134–143.)

MATERIAL RESOURCES

These types of resources range from money, to specific pieces of equipment, and opportunities to develop and test out new ways of being. Most worthwhile endeavours will carry a cost, which may be hefty. It may be in terms of money, time, personal effects, provisions or material resources. The cost of realizing your individual potential may come as a surprise.

Before you can consider self-actualization you will need to have acquired the ability to survive and maintain yourself. It is important that you seek out or create the material and economic resources you need. Do not sit around waiting for these resources to appear or complain that they do not exist.

★ TRY THIS NOW!

Draw a map with yourself in the centre. Then draw lines to represent the people in your life. How close and important their relationship is to you is represented by the distance which you place them from yourself.

You will have some commitments to and expectations of each

person. See if you can identify what these are. Equally, they will probably have expectations of and commitments to you. You may want to write these down and check them out with the people involved. It is likely that these people will be affected by any changes you wish to make.

Clarifying your commitments and expectations will give you a basis for negotiating the support that you need from a position of mutual understanding.

Of the people in your map, who is supportive or could be supportive of you as you are and of you as

you would like to be? What kind of support do they give you?

For example, do they give you support for your internal life, or for external activity? Can these people give you the kind of support you need, or will you have to look outside your present circle?

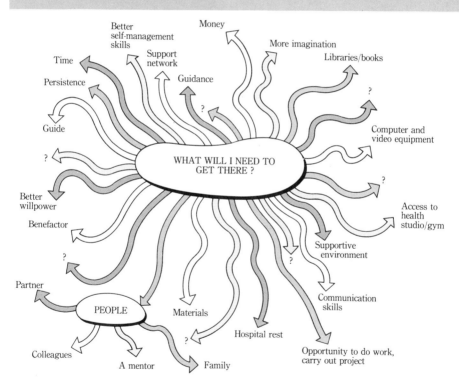

★ TEST YOURSELF!

Create a branch pattern that outlines all the resources you will need on your

journey. Indicate which of these are essential or simply useful, which you

already have at your disposal, and which you need immediately and which you will

need later. Ask for comments from a friend or expert.

It is important to get a clear sense and image of what you are aiming for before you put all your energy into realizing it, just as an architect makes a drawing and/or a model of a building before it is built.

This serves three purposes. First, alterations and adjustments can be made in the light of the drawing. Second, it is easier to see the likely difficulties in construction. Third, it creates enthusiasm and generates interest in getting the building completed. You need to do this for your goal.

MAKING YOUR MODEL

When you have been through the various previous stages you will have a good idea of the direction in which you want to go, how to get there, and the practical difficulties involved in the journey. You may find that it is not, in fact, what you wanted.

All this needs to be synthesized and made more real through your creation of a model of yourself as you could be. This model will guide you or draw you forward toward your goal.

As you spend time visualizing your idea you unleash the motivation and power of the image. This, in turn, triggers your emotions and your desire to get moving into action.

It is important to allow yourself regular time to dream and imagine what it and you will be like when you get there. Repeating the images will strengthen your resolve and your commitment. Making an affirmation, that is a statement to yourself which reinforces your position and direction, will also add weight to your commitment.

ENCOUNTERING INTERNAL RESISTANCE

You cannot impose your will in the face of opposition from the rest of your internal community. You may find that you cannot sustain the images if you begin to experience excessive fear or resistance to your ideal. You then need to accept these feelings and blockages and integrate them.

Repressing them, ignoring them, or trying to impose your will on them will only create internal rebellion. You may fall prey to your internal saboteur. When you encounter these internal resistances, it is important not to fight them but to maintain a permissive, accepting attitude toward them.

Change or moving toward the unknown is challenging and risky. If you are prepared for the likelihood of difficulty you will not be so disheartened when it comes.

If you can maintain an open accepting attitude throughout your imagining and subsequent action you will gradually find a way of quieting or integrating the opposing factors to your idea.

This may require patience and persistence. It is as important not to let the negative members of your internal community take over as it is to gain their cooperation.

CREATING YOUR IMAGE

As you create your image in this way you may find yourself moving back and forth between the stages in mapping your life. This imaging will enable you to build up the positive psychological voltage necessary for the realization of your idea.

When creating your image or ideal it is important to use as many different ways of creating and amplifying your vision of the future as you find you need. You may wish to paint, draw, write, keep a diary, interpret your dreams or read biographies or books.

This is in addition to your own imaginative evocation, especially of your behaviour as it might be at the end of the process. When you have created the images of your ideal make sure they are kept in prominent places externally and that you evoke them in your imagination regularly. This will help you to make use of the powerful effect which images can have on you.

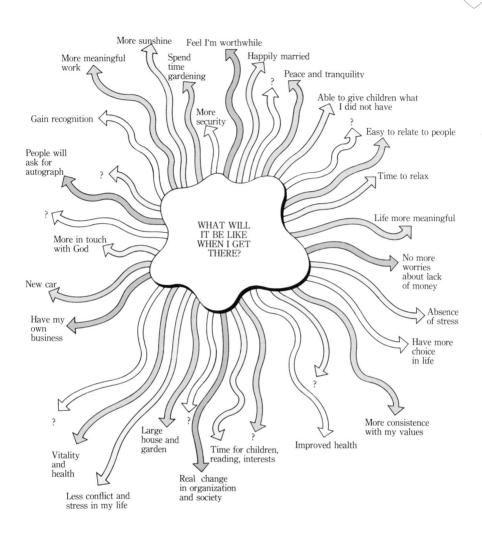

TRY THIS NOW!

Before you put your ideas and plans into action try to imagine what your life will be like when you have attained your goal.

If this is a major change in your life, you may wish to create your ideal model or image over a period of time, refining your goal further each time you return to it.

The next stage is to get rid of any false or impossible ideals. Be critical of your plans. Ask someone you trust to play devil's advocate to test your clarity and commitment.

Finally, when you are clear that your vision of the future is the one you want to commit yourself to, imagine what it would be like not to reach your vision. Then spend some time identifying the benefits of reaching your desired goal. This will help increase your motivation for moving into action.

Your self-esteem is the level of belief you have in yourself and an indication of your level of self-acceptance. It is a way of measuring how worthwhile you judge yourself to be, and a way of monitoring your psychological well-being.

Self-esteem is often linked with the way in which you see yourself, that is, your self-image, and is related to concepts such as self-confidence and self-respect. If asked 'How do you see yourself?' you may draw a complete blank, or you may come up with a list of vital statistics, geographical information and occupational details such as 'I am 33, 5'10", and have brown eyes and brown hair. I am married with two children and live in Guildford, where I work as a teacher'.

These facts do not describe who you really are or how you feel about yourself. Self-esteem, and self-image, go far beyond just your skills and abilities. Your physical characteristics and your activities may not necessarily reflect things you have chosen for yourself; equally, they may not be a true representation of your unique identity.

Self-esteem plays a vital part in how you live your life and the depth of satisfaction and joy you experience in learning, working and playing. However, your level of self-esteem is variable. It changes as you relate to the sense of well-being within yourself, and in response to your interaction with the environment, including other people. It can be raised by giving yourself appreciation and by receiving recognition and praise from others.

Having a healthy level of self-esteem does not mean that you are a perfect person with no room for change and review. You can still make mistakes, but at least you will not feel destroyed when you do, or when someone gives you negative criticism.

HOW DO YOU SEE YOURSELF?

Your self-image is how you see yourself rather than a reflection of how others see you or how you would like to be. It radically affects your self-esteem. It is difficult to change, since it is set very early in life by the valuing and devaluing messages you received from those around you.

A negative self-image can be a crippling handicap, and can inhibit your ability to relate to other people. A healthy self-image, on the other hand, is a precious commodity.

People with a good self-image see themselves as being liked, wanted, able, worthy, acceptable, as having choices and being capable of understanding. More importantly, they behave as though they were all these.

Although difficult to change, your self-image can be altered in a variety of ways so that it can be consolidated into a more healthy reflection of your true self. You do not need to remain trapped in a prison of negative self-image. The belief that change is possible, plus a little determination, will set you on your way to improving your self-image and maintaining a healthy level of self-esteem.

★ TRY THIS NOW!

Think back to a time when you felt really valued and worthwhile, even if it was only for a short time. Then remember a time when you felt devalued and worthless. Try to capture the fullness of both these experiences.

Now, imagine a scale running from one to ten, with one signifying feelings of worthlessness and ten feelings of value.

Review the experiences of the past day/week and place them on this scale to rate your level of self-worth for each situation.

What does this show you about your general level of respect and value for yourself? Does this correspond with what you believe about your value and how you usually experience your worth?

Imagine a Martian watching you, making a list of your behaviours, traits, qualities and attitudes. Write out this list.

Which would you like to have known and which not? Note those you take delight in but keep quiet about and those you find most difficult to accept.

How do you feel when they are exposed, and how do you react?

★ REMEMBER!

People with a healthy self-image:
● Have certain values and principles they believe in strongly. And they are willing to defend and/or modify these as necessary.
● Are capable of acting on their best judgement without feeling excessively guilty or regretful, even when such feelings are appropriate.

● Do not spend undue time fretting about mistakes, being upset by experiences or worrying about tomorrow.
● Retain confidence in their ability to deal with problems in the face of setbacks and failures.
● Feel equal to others as persons irrespective of differences in skills, status or background.
● Believe that they are persons of interest and value.
● Can accept praise without false modesty or guilt.
● Can accept and admit to a wide range of emotions.
● Are sensitive to the needs of other people and to their own needs.
● Can resist domination by others.
● Are capable of being kind, and tend to look for the best in others.

IF YOU DO NOT FEEL GOOD ABOUT YOURSELF

● It is more difficult to make contact with other people.
● It is more difficult, and more energy- and time-consuming, to make decisions that are right for you. It is also more difficult to bring these decisions into practice.
● The world around you can feel hostile and unsafe.
● It is difficult to hear the messages telling you that other people love and appreciate you.
● You spend a lot of time being anxious and worrying about what other people think of you.

IF YOU FEEL GOOD ABOUT YOURSELF

● You feel energetic and alive.
● You believe more in your own competence.
● You feel that you can try to solve problems when they arise because you are more confident that you can do your best.
● You have so much more to give other people, and are much more free with your appreciation of others.
● You are more open to feedback and suggestions from others, and more willing to accept criticism and suggestions for change.

You tend to draw your self-esteem from a sense of your own values, that is, the qualities you use to judge yourself and others. People often value what they are good at and devalue what they consider themselves to be poor at. A low rating on a quality that you do not value will have little effect on your self-esteem, whereas a high or low rating on a quality that you do value will have a significant effect.

Self-esteem is maintained and supported by selectively interpreting facts, standards and situations. It depends not just on how good you are but how good you want to be. Most people tend to select goals within their range of realizable accomplishments. However, some people set impossible goals and this usually has a devastating effect on their self-esteem.

A great deal of positive self-esteem seems to exist where people can make choices. This explains why people who have limited choice are more likely to have chronic low self-esteem, which is often called an inferiority complex. Of course, everybody feels inferior in some ways. Equally it is possible for us all to feel worthwhile, by defining our own values, friends, work and possessions where we can. All the choices you make about these things are potential resources for building and maintaining self-esteem.

★ TEST YOURSELF!

First, describe yourself as you think you should be and write it down. Next, write down what you like and dislike about yourself.

Now, ask a close friend to describe what they value most and least about you.

Compare the three descriptions. Are they similar or widely dissonant? What do you learn about yourself from comparing them? How do you feel about yourself in the light of your discoveries?

YOUR FALSE SELF

A healthy level of self-esteem comes from unconditional self-acceptance, from caring for and loving yourself. Getting to know yourself, though, is much more difficult than you may think. Even in the healthiest of people this 'self' keeps changing as you grow.

We all develop what might be determined a 'false' self, a mask or a front that we present to the world to protect our true self, which may be vulnerable and undeveloped.

This front usually consists of an image of how we think others want us to be. This is sometimes called your adapted self, since you have altered your true self to conform to the expectations and desires of others. You probably did this to gain love from those who are important for your survival.

Another common reason that you, literally, pretend to be someone else is that you may have an ideal image of who or what you would like to be but have not yet become. This is a necessary growth process, but may cause problems if the ideal you choose is unrealistic and impossible to achieve. You may then over-identify with your ideal at the expense of your true self and become alienated from the person you truly are.

Your true self cannot ever be totally buried, and you are often painfully aware that it is inside you somewhere.

Because your self-image is bound up with your adaptive self, you are not fully in touch with your true self and your true potential. The more you try to live up to and by the standards and expectations of others, the more you feel that you are not who you should be, and this pretence may result in severe anxiety.

YOUR TRUE SELF

At conception, your true self is just a seed with the potential to grow and develop, both physically and psychologically. As with all seeds your true self needs careful attention if it is to blossom. Growing up is full of hazards and challenges, and you may not get the support and attention you need to develop your true self.

Unconditional acceptance is the most fundamental part of this care as far as your self-esteem is concerned. This encourages you to be yourself and gives you the courage to make yourself known to others, which in turn helps you to get to know yourself.

However, in this state you are open and vulnerable. It is not surprising, therefore, that you develop ways of defending yourself by constructing your false self.

When you are in this vulnerable state you are particularly susceptible to receiving and believing negative messages. These messages devalue you, teach you to believe you are not worthwhile as yourself, and create your negative self.

As children, in particular, people do not understand why these messages occur and tend to assume there is something wrong with them if they are not given considerable acceptance and understanding by others. These negative messages tend to overwhelm any positive messages that are received by you.

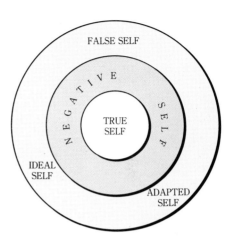

When you are first trying to let go of your false self-image, you must again experience and evaluate these negative messages before you can get in touch with your true self. Do not be surprised if, at first, your self-esteem becomes lowered as you make this exploration. This is usually a sign that you are working through your 'negative self-image' layer to get to your core, your true self.

SELF-ESTEEM FLUCTUATES

Self-esteem is drawn from a number of areas. If you have a healthy level of self-esteem you will draw on all of these areas without being overdependent on any single one.

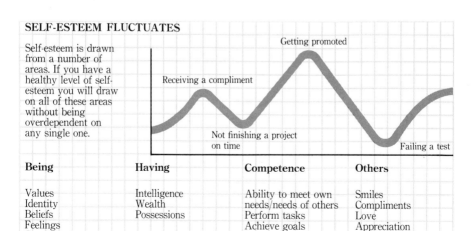

Being	Having	Competence	Others
Values	Intelligence	Ability to meet own	Smiles
Identity	Wealth	needs/needs of others	Compliments
Beliefs	Possessions	Perform tasks	Love
Feelings		Achieve goals	Appreciation
Constructs		Pass tests	

As you grew up you received messages from parents, teachers and peers which have affected your self-esteem. These messages are both positive and negative, and help to shape your image of yourself.

They may reinforce the positive aspects of your character and personality, but more often they remind you of what may need changing, which results in a lowering of your self-esteem.

★ TEST YOURSELF!

Think of times when your sense of self-worth was low, perhaps when you felt despondent and unlovable. Write down precisely what it was that caused your self-worth to deteriorate. For example, it might have been caused by a relationship, work, your health or your family. Write down as many situations as you can remember.

How did you feel, and what did you decide about yourself on those occasions? Do you see any patterns emerging?

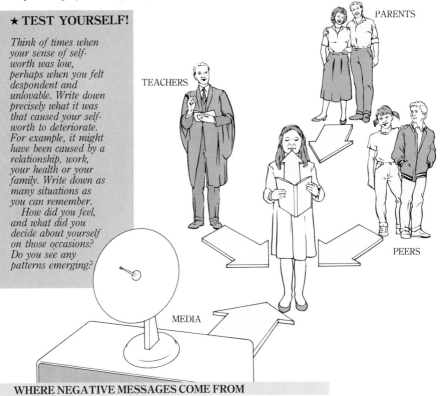

PARENTS

TEACHERS

PEERS

MEDIA

WHERE NEGATIVE MESSAGES COME FROM

Life so often puts you in touch with what is not good about you. As a child, this may have meant your parents or family criticized your hopes and dreams. They may have told you that you were silly for wanting to do something that meant a lot to you.

As an adult, you are constantly being criticized. You receive a constant stream of messages about your abilities and innate capacities, which aim to demean them. This often happens as part of social games, when the ability to humiliate others is thought of as having a sense of humour. However playful the statements may seem, you may still feel put down.

You also receive negative messages from the media. We live in a highly image-conscious world, and it is easy to become a victim to the expectations and norms around you.

How you see yourself is often as a comparison to images presented to you by television, films, magazines and high street windows. This may make you feel that you are not quite up to the mark, but that is how advertising works. It relies on generating sensations of inadequacy so that you will feel the need to spend money on improving yourself.

These negative messages are heard over and over again. As a result, you tend to take in these messages and internalize them, so that they become a part of you. And, in addition, you rarely try to counteract these negative messages with positive ones for fear of being told that you are being conceited.

THE EFFECTS OF NEGATIVE MESSAGES

The constant absorption of negative messages may mean that you lose contact with your own abilities, and that your true self gets buried deep inside you. This is because you are living up to the expectations of others and seeking their approval rather than doing things to please yourself. This might mean, for example, that you entered into a certain profession in order to get parental approval rather than choosing one for yourself.

If you are not in touch with your true self, you may feel that somewhere there is something missing in your life. You may have little energy for the activities that should be enjoyable, or you may have recurring bad moods that seem out of proportion with the circumstances that brought them on.

The sentiments of a sales manager sum up another aspect of the problem. 'I set out to be successful, to have a nice house, a big car and enough money to educate my children well. I am now 40, and I have all of those things, and yet I am not happy. I really do not understand it. Is there something wrong with me?'

This is not an uncommon feeling. Part of you is always in contact with the hopes, dreams and desires that you have buried, and somewhere deep inside you may feel unfulfilled and isolated. At worst, you may become indifferent to yourself and to others.

The lower your self-esteem becomes the less you care about yourself. Your motivation for change may become low, and you may feel resentful and judgemental toward those whose lives have taken a different course.

The secret of satisfaction is finding your own true path, in being in touch with and acting on your own individuality. Most people go through stages in their lives during which their level of self-esteem and their ability to get in touch with their true feelings changes. This is a common occurrence and a natural dynamic of existence.

What is important to know is that you *can* shift the balance and break out of any possible destructive cycles that may keep your level of self-esteem low – lower, in fact, than you may even be aware.

Explicit	Tacit
'You never do anything right'.	Being ignored
	Eye contact avoided
'Why are you always so slow?'	

The messages you receive can be either explicit or tacit. Explicit messages are spoken messages; they are usually clearly and precisely expressed. Tacit messages are expressed without words, often implied by body language or attitude.

★ TRY THIS NOW!

To identify the messages that currently influence your behaviour, complete the following statements. Try to write down as many possible endings as you can for each.

I should/should not

I must/must not

I have to/ought to

Can you identify who these messages came from, such as parents, siblings or teachers? Which of these messages enhance your feelings of self-worth?

Decide which of these messages you are going to keep as yours and which you are going to discard. Then change the 'shoulds' into 'coulds', 'musts' into 'mights', and 'have tos' into 'choose tos'. This will help you be more conscious of the fact that you do have choice.

★ REMEMBER!

● *Everybody needs love and approval.*
● *Love and approval are often withheld by others if you do not live up to their expectations or meet their needs.*
● *When these are withheld you may compromise your true self to get the love and approval you so need and deserve.*
● *If you come to expect disapproval you may, consciously or unconsciously, give up and decide that it is easier to live up to the expectations of others than be true to your real self.*

The emphasis in Western society is on decisions, actions and results. By concentrating on these, you can often lose sight of who you really are and what you really want out of life. To balance your life you also need to pay attention to, and accept, your feelings and your body, so that you can get in touch with your true, whole self.

FIND OUT WHO YOU ARE

The first step in raising your self-esteem is to look at yourself realistically. This means working out who you are now, rather than imagining yourself as you would like to be. You need to look at the relationship between what you believe about yourself, how you think you should be, and what you are actually feeling.

For example, you might think that you are efficient and alert. However, there are times when you feel unproductive and confused, although you think you should be efficient all the time. As soon as this happens you will probably experience an internal battle, which occurs when you give yourself one message and feel another.

In general, people internalize messages and information about themselves, both positive and negative. However, it is often the more negative messages that really make an impression. By absorbing these negative messages you create an internal dictator who tells you not to make mistakes, pull your socks up, pull yourself together and to keep a stiff upper lip.

This dictator may keep telling you who you should be or what you should be doing, but it is not in touch with what you are actually feeling. Often, it keeps

repeating the negative messages you have internalized, such as 'You're not good enough. There you are, you've done it again'. As a result of these constant internal battles you may experience a deadening of your emotions and energy.

★ TRY THIS NOW!

Recall the times when you felt really good about yourself. What specifically enabled you to achieve this state? It may be something to do with your work, your family, your achievements or your possessions.

Do you notice any patterns emerging? How can you make use of these sources more effectively?

What blocks you from accepting yourself? Imagine this block: What does it look like? Draw it.

Imagine you are the block. How do you feel? Imagine you have overcome the block. What does it feel like?

Now converse with the block, playing both parts and negotiating until a workable compromise is agreed.

★ REMEMBER!

● *Reinforce the positive messages you receive. Tell yourself you are a caring, intelligent, attractive and worthy human being. Write these statements down, and put them where you can see them every day.*
● *Start thinking differently about yourself and appreciate yourself on a daily basis.*

● *Remind yourself of what has gone well each day. Take pride in your accomplishments and achievements, no matter how small.*
● *Avoid people who put you down, or learn to confront them.*
● *Take care of yourself by looking after your appearance. And give yourself treats—you deserve it.*

RECOGNIZE THE PATTERNS

These negative internal messages do not come in isolation. They are often a part of a 'pattern', and are invariably linked with your past. A pattern arises when one incident triggers you off into a whole range of emotions, behaviours and actions which may cause you to feel out of control. These emotions and actions often take place automatically, and you may be aware of thinking 'I've done it again. I've been here before. Why am I doing this?'

If, for example, you were told as a child, either explicitly or tacitly, that you were not creative, this probably will have caused some pain. And in your life now, if people ask you to do something creative, or criticize you when you are being creative, you may again feel that pain, which triggers off a pattern of feelings.

When you fall into the pattern there are a number of different responses you might have. You may become defensive, aggressive, depressed or low in energy. Another common response is that, as a result of feeling worthless or inferior, you might overcompensate and become boastful or brag about your accomplishments.

If you continue to

You're not creative

Please do something creative

accept the negative messages and denigrate yourself, you are less likely to be tolerant of hearing the successes and good news of other people. You may perceive their news as bragging and boasting, even when it is not.

There are ways in which you can interrupt these internal destructive cycles. The first vital step is to be aware of your internal voice and past messages about yourself that have caused you distress. Stop for a minute and think about the messages your internal voice gives you. Notice anything that communicates itself concerning your emotions, your body or your abilities.

TRUST YOUR EMOTIONS

Another way of breaking destructive cycles is to start accepting your emotions. There is so much information within yourself that you do not listen to, that you deny or are not even aware of.

Human emotions are often seen as a necessary evil. In reality your feelings, both positive and negative, are a great source of information about yourself. Also, by listening to and being aware of your emotions you will create much more impetus and energy to deal with whatever is at hand.

For example, if you are asked by a colleague to do a certain task you may *think* 'yes' because you dare not say 'no' – you may even end up saying 'yes'. However, you *feel* 'no' as a gut reaction.

Listening to your gut reaction does not necessarily mean that you will not do the task, but it could be an indication that you need more time to consider the request, or to demand certain conditions.

Trusting your emotions places you in a better position to negotiate a solution you feel comfortable with. If you do not recognize and work with your emotions, the more you deny a central part of yourself.

LISTEN TO YOUR BODY

It is important to bring this awareness of yourself to your body. Like your emotions, your body can provide you with a considerable amount of information about what you really feel or need. Minor aches and pains, body temperature and illness can tell you a number of things about what you are truly feeling.

In reviewing your self-esteem it is important to review your relationship with your body. How do you treat it? How do you look after it? Do you get enough exercise? Do you have a healthy diet? The better you treat your body, the more you will respect yourself.

Try to listen to yourself and trust yourself more. If you deny your emotions and your body, the greater the internal battle becomes. Respecting your emotions and your body, as well as your thoughts, means respecting yourself as a whole person.

Try to be a friend to yourself, and look after yourself. It is especially important to give yourself love and appreciation, or to ask others for it, particularly if you feel yourself entering a negative cycle.

How you feel about yourself affects the qualities of your relationships with others. If you feel bad about yourself, it will be more difficult for you to reach out to others – and at the same time much more difficult to let other people into your life.

If your self-esteem is low you will not easily attract other people because the way in which you project yourself is tacitly picked up by others. This could mean that in your personal life you find it difficult to make or maintain friendships. If you feel that you are not an interesting or worthy person, other people will be able to sense this. They will have a difficult time finding you interesting or worthy, even if they think you are. Feeling that you are not worth caring for or not worth loving makes it difficult for others to let you know they do care for you, and difficult for you to take their feelings seriously.

In your working life you may find that you are not taken seriously or your opinions are not listened to. If you want to ask for a pay rise or additional responsibilities at work, you will need to let your superiors know that you are worth the extra money and capable of performing the additional duties – they may know this, but you also need to believe it yourself.

If you feel badly about yourself you may find it difficult to have honest relationships with others. If you are too worried about what others think of you, you may find that your feelings are hurt easily, that you take offence at other people's comments. When you feel good about yourself you will feel more relaxed about your relationships. You will be less concerned about what others might be thinking or saying, and people will listen to you and take you seriously. When you respect yourself, others will too.

LEARN TO COMMUNICATE

It is often assumed that communication should come naturally when, in fact, we are often ill-prepared to relate clearly and directly with others. You may find it difficult to express your feelings and to let others know what you want and need.

Or, you may hesitate to ask others what they think or feel about you for fear that they will criticize you, or that you will not be able to handle their negative feelings. You may be afraid they will tell you things you do not want to hear.

As a result of this hesitation and fear, our opinions and feelings about each other either stay hidden, or are expressed in indirect ways. You can learn skills that will enable you to communicate with others while still respecting yourself and them.

★ TEST YOURSELF!

Try to imagine yourself as others see you. Choose a friend who knows you well and whom you trust. Write down how you imagine they would describe you to someone else. Now check your comments with them – how do they see you?

Consider the people you have around you, including your family, workmates, friends and acquaintances. Write down the ways in which they contribute to your self-esteem, or detract from it.

What are the most and least valuable contributions to your self-esteem? Is there a way you can ensure the more positive ones occur more often? Or can you interrupt the negative? Who contributes the most to your self-esteem? Can you spend more time with these people?

THE IMPORTANCE OF FEEDBACK

It is important to learn to ask for and receive feedback if you are to understand yourself. Here are some strategies that may help you to ask for and receive feedback from a superior or colleague.

● **Negative assertion**
Make a negative statement about yourself. It might be that you have made a mistake at work, or have felt in low spirits lately.

● **Negative inquiry**
Invite negative feedback about your behaviour, actions, decisions or moods. For example, you might tell your superiors that you are aware you have been late for appointments twice this week. Ask if they are annoyed with you.

● **Positive assertion and positive inquiry**
State something positive that is happening for you, or invite positive feedback.

● **Open inquiry**
Ask an open question about yourself, for example, ask a colleague what he thinks about your performance.

● **Receiving negative feedback**
Notice when you feel the criticism is valid, invalid, manipulative or a direct put-down. If the criticism is valid, try to accept it without becoming defensive or making lengthy explanations.

● **Receiving positive feedback**
Breathe in and accept it. Do not feel that you have to find a return compliment. Just say thank you. And remember that it is as important to give feedback to others as well as to receive it.

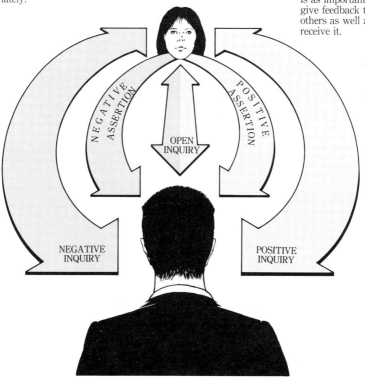

If you are just starting out on your career, wanting to develop your current career or, for whatever reason, considering changing to another, you have a critical choice to make. You can drift along and let your circumstances and the opportunities that arise determine which path you take. Or you can begin to take charge and gain control over your future. To do this, you will need to develop a career map to enable you to gain insights into your potential and direction.

MAKING THE DECISION

Many individuals, while experiencing some periods of stability and relative equilibrium in their lives and careers, may also become aware that something is missing, or that there is a lack of synchronization or direction.

This feeling may be heightened by external factors, such as failure to be promoted, redundancy, change in family commitments, or the necessity to uproot and move to a new location. It may also arise through imminent retirement, or internal factors such as being conscious of time running out, a sense of stagnation, or feeling frustrated or burned out.

People who are suffering from career 'problems' of this kind notice others who appear happy, fulfilled and successful. These people may not necessarily be successful in conventional career terms of having climbed the work ladder and achieved financial reward. Many are just as fulfilled and successful having decided to change the direction of their lives completely.

Such people may have moved laterally within a career path rather than up, or even moved away from a career altogether, seeing a job as a small and transitional part of their life. The one common link between these people is their decision to choose for themselves the direction they wish to take.

Whether you are starting out on a career, want to develop your current job, need to consider a career move, or are questioning your current work/job, you too have a choice. You can drift along and let chance determine your future, or you can begin to be successful in taking charge of yourself and gaining control over your own destiny.

At a time when the rate of technological change is so rapid, when whole areas of employment can shift, when the pattern and shape of the working day is altering, you now may need to rethink where you are going. You will need to look at all the possibilities, including retraining, to develop your potential more fully and rechannel your efforts in new areas.

LEARNING NEW SKILLS

You might think that you are too old to make any major career changes, particularly those that require new skills and qualifications. But most people who are 'over the hill' are those who have chosen to be that way.

There are many thousands of mature students enrolled in college courses all over the country. Some seek self-understanding, some want higher degrees in their current careers, while others are training for change or second careers. Still others are fulfilling a long suppressed curiosity about the world and the people in it.

Certainly it may be more difficult to learn skills that require specific physical strengths, but this is not as much of a deterrent as you may think, since there are schemes specifically designed for training the older worker.

One practical note worth remembering is to find out whether or not opportunities exist for you to use the skills you learn. You may find it necessary to work in a part-time job with a lower salary, or do voluntary work in order to utilize those skills that you cannot use in full-time employment.

THE NEED FOR PLANNING

If you decide to take charge of your own life with regard to your career, you will need to sit down and do some planning. Most people have planning skills but seldom apply them to their personal lives.

You are probably involved in planning activities in one form or another, even though you may not realize it. From production plans at work to budgeting your family's expenditure, you often use your abilities to assess future needs and consequently ensure that resources will be available when they are needed.

A prerequisite to planning is, of course, the need to decide what it is you want to achieve. For any career change to be successful, you will need to determine what your goals are, both long and short term. And you will need to develop some specific plans toward achieving these.

If you are willing to take the time to use a systematic approach to career planning you will need to consider the skills that you have or might need to develop (including both the things you do well and enjoy, or would like to do better), as well as your life values and

the context within which you work or want to work. The difficulty most people have is knowing where to start and how to gather the necessary data.

There are a number of steps you can work through to help you overcome these difficulties. These include determining:
● Where you have been, to help you to gain insights from reviewing your past experiences and achievements.
● Where you are now, to help you identify your work preferences, and the skills and values you find important.
● Where you are

going, which will help you create a realistic vision of the future, discover your potential, set goals and work out a plan of action.

Once you have systematically worked these through you will have a clearer idea of your career direction, a realistic view of the options open to you, and achievable goals which incorporate insights you have gained into your potential.

This vision will open up a new channel through which you can feel committed to take a positive, active approach to yourself and your career.

★ REMEMBER!

Life is always full of risks, but it is also full of opportunities. If you do not look at these opportunities

and start discovering the unknown, then the risks can never be evaluated in terms of the pay off, that is,

the benefits you could reap. Do not feel that the career you have, and what you know, although

unsatisfactory, is better than the unknown.

For many people, life and career are integrated parts of a single whole. Many of the aspects that concern you regarding your life, such as your values, preferences and assumptions of the demands that will be made of you in the future, reflect on how you work, and how you view work itself.

These aspects will, in turn, have been influenced by your past experiences. Rediscovering these experiences, and assessing their quality, is the first step toward gaining insights into the patterns or trends in your personal development to date.

WHAT DID YOU ENJOY?

Start by looking back over your previous experiences and try to remember some of the times when you were doing something that you enjoyed, which stretched your capabilities and imagination, and which gave you a real sense of satisfaction.

These may have been short- or long-term activities, routine or unusual, and include both work and leisure activities. Scan your school years, hobbies and interests. For example, you might think about:
● A project you undertook.
● A room you decorated.
● An article you wrote.
● A boat you built.
● A course of study you enjoyed.
● A holiday you initiated.

● A business you set up.
Or it may have been a role you were assigned that involved:
● Chairing a meeting.
● Presenting a paper.
● Designing a programme.
● Leading a sports team.
● Being involved in a community or social club.
The above are only examples that might help trigger some ideas for you. Remember, it does not have to be dramatic, public, spectacular or newsworthy. What is important is that it was something you found extremely satisfying and fulfilling. Try to remember between 6 and 10 situations if possible, so that you can obtain sufficient information to enable you to work on in the next stage.

★ REMEMBER!

This is your past you are reviewing, and in the final analysis it will be your list and contain the categories that have the most meaning for you. Do

not be constrained by the above suggestions; they are intended merely as a guide.

When you complete this review, look back over the lists you have

compiled and reflect on any patterns or trends and preferences that you notice.

It might be tempting to start to

draw conclusions now, and to think about acting upon any insights you have gained. But there is further data to collect and work through.

WHAT DID YOU VALUE?

Now take each situation in turn and break it down into its component parts. Try to relive it in every detail, remembering where you were, what you were doing, who else was there, how you felt and what the results of the activity were.

Write this information down on a large sheet of paper. The exercises require you to be open to all outcomes and not feel constrained by lack of space. Let your mind wander freely and do not censor your thoughts nor be afraid to feel good or proud about your experience.

For each situation list:

What the environment was
● Indoors or out.
● Open or enclosed space.
● Town or country.
● Sea or mountains.
● Quiet or noisy.

What type of activity it was
● Involved with people.
● Dealing with information, data or ideas.
● Working with things such as machinery, or materials such as wood or metal.

What the relationships were
● If you were with others, were you collaborative, competitive, distant?

Your role and responsibility
● An ideas person, a coordinator, an evaluator.
● A leader or follower.

What your level of responsibility was

What type of skills you used
● Manual or non-manual.
● Communication skills, including written, oral, observation or listening.

What knowledge you needed
● Financial, environmental, business information or technical.

What were the circumstances
● What support did you get or need?
● Where did it come from?
● Were you acting under pressure? If so, how much, where did it come from?
● What recognition did you receive, if any? How important was this to your achievement of the activity?
● What was it about the activity that you enjoyed most?
● What did you value most?

PETER'S PROGRESS

It may be helpful to look at Peter's progress as you work through your own career map.

Peter had spent the past 12 years in sales and had developed into a highly competent computer salesman.

At the age of 35 he had felt very pleased with the way he had been able to balance the emotional and financial demands of having a young family with the work pressure to improve targets and maintain his technical expertise in an ever-changing industry.

The irregular, long work hours and resultant lack of time to maintain his active sports life had, he felt, been a justifiable sacrifice in achieving career progression.

Two years ago his company underwent a structural reorganization based on a movement toward a customer 'total service strategy'. Whereas previously Peter was primarily responsible for providing compatible software, his job now required highly developed skills in customer relations and an in-depth understanding of the business. In addition, his customer base had changed and, geographically, was centred in inner London, which meant far more time spent commuting.

Closer integration with the head office and other members of the regional sales team required frequent meetings and a capacity to work jointly on projects. While these seemed to Peter a useful forum for support, the time taken at these sessions left little, if any, to devote to maintaining his technical competence by keeping up-to-date with all the new technological changes.

Peter began to realize that technological changes were not the only things he had to cope with. He was feeling less and less competent, and more isolated from his colleagues. Now, nearing 38 years of age, he had lost his sense of career direction and was unsure of what he could do to stop the growing feeling of being stuck.

Since life is a continuously moving flow of experiences and opportunities, it would be naïve to think that your earlier choice in terms of your job or career is necessarily the right one for you now. Not only may your external circumstances have changed, such as your level of independence, personal finances, family commitments or professional requirements, but your internal circumstances may also have changed. These may include your likes and dislikes, your feelings about yourself and others, and the way you prefer to spend your time.

It is necessary to keep up-to-date with yourself. You need to build up a self-inventory of where you are now. This involves looking at three different aspects of yourself; what you like and dislike about

ANALYSE YOUR PRESENT JOB

Work through your present job and your feelings about it, as Peter did. Start by listing what you like and dislike about your present work situation. Try to list 10 items for each list.

You now need to determine what it is that you prefer about work. Use whatever categories are appropriate for you.

Your likes	Peter's likes
	Reading journals.
	Having time to myself to think.
	Making calls on clients.
	Drawing up the day's activities.
	Sorting through the post.
	Confirming a contract.
	Working out my bonus.

Routine	Ambiguity and change
Immediate results	Don't mind waiting
Careful planner	Risk taker
Thinker	Doer
Talker	Listener
Likes pressure	Prefers less pressure
Intuitively	Analytically
In a team	Alone
Large organization	Small organization
Initiating	Building on other's idea
Narrowly defined areas	Broadly based areas

Then determine what it is you dislike about your present job. Write your list down, including what makes you unhappy, and which activities you would avoid if you could.

Your dislikes	Peter's dislikes
	Commuting.
	Lengthy planning meetings.
	Weekly staff meetings.
	Administrative paperwork.
	Waiting for information.
	Studying business manuals.

Your preferences	Peter's preferences
	Some ambiguity
	Fairly immediate results
	Moderate risktaker
	Doer
	Talker
	Moderate pressure
	Analytically
	Alone
	No preference
	Initiating
	Narrowly defined

your present job, what your preferences are, and the values you hold regarding the context of your day-to-day activities. The rationale for reviewing your life in this way can be illustrated by looking at Peter's situation alongside your own.

Another area to clarify is whether you prefer working	with things, data and information, or people, or both.

Things/data/ information	**People**
Designing	Consulting
Reporting	Leading
Drawing	Following
Machines/tools	Servicing
Writing	Teamwork
Deciphering	Negotiating
Abstracts	Helping
	Selling

Your list	**Peter's list**
	Designing (things)
	Drawing (things)
	Selling (people)
	Negotiating (people)

Already Peter's lists have highlighted a number of issues. Although he likes meeting clients and working out his own schedules, he also prefers more 'doing' – and with fairly immediate results. He also prefers some ambiguity, and although he is analytical in his approach to his work, he does not like long-term strategic planning meetings, particularly when the outcomes are so interdependent on his peers.

Thus, you can see that some of the aspects of your working life that you may like or dislike may run counter to the way in which you prefer to work.

DETERMINE THE CONDITIONS

There is one final aspect to incorporate into your present day self-inventory. You need to determine under what conditions you work most effectively, that is, the surroundings or circumstances that are really important to you. Note that you may not have these conditions now, you may just want them.

Refer back to the headings you used when looking at your past experiences if you need a trigger mechanism. Consider, for example:

- Relationships at work.
- Atmosphere.
- Environment.
- Constraint/scope.

Assess your skills
For some people, the perception of themselves is narrow and self-limiting, and a consequence of feeling 'stuck' and unskilled in some way at the moment, as Peter felt.

One way of breaking through this and creating a broader, fuller picture of what you can do is the following. Take a large sheet of paper and write down the broadest possible range of skills, talents, abilities, strengths and resources you possess. Use these guidelines:

- Put aside fears of being boastful and egocentric or proud.
- Do not evaluate or censor your thoughts.
- Consider the past and present, and what you might be able to do or would like to learn.
- Look for hidden potential.

It may help you if you ask someone else to tell you what they regard as your skills and talents. This could, perhaps, be a close colleague, a trusted friend who has known you for a long time, or your partner.

Categorize the list in terms of:
- Types of skills required, including manual, intellectual, organizational, managerial, aesthetic, artistic.
- Whether your skills in these areas are highly developed or underdeveloped.
- Whether you have hidden potential in these areas.
- In the context of carrying out your job, have your values changed? Have you outgrown your previous values?
- Are your values and preferences in the way you work frustrated by the path you are on? If so, how?
- What abilities do you have which have not been put to use as often as you would like? Which skills and talents would you like to develop more fully?

Reflection upon these, and upon any additional issues which have come up for you now, allows you to progress toward looking at the future and what you hope to achieve in your career.

Before you can get to where you want to be in terms of your job and career, you must determine your goals or objectives. Before you can achieve your ambition, you will need to work out what it is you are aiming for. Think of this as your 'overall life mission', which will be some overriding statement of intent, or main ambition.

It is critical to become aware of this goal so that you can begin to act more consis- tently to accomplish it. If you are unaware of what your goal is, it is likely that at times you will act without thinking and so defeat your own purpose. Your goal for the future can take any form, and will clearly be idiosyncratic. It may be that your goal is to serve others, teach others, make a name for yourself, be a leader, have adventures, have power or control of others, enjoy yourself, make money or build a secure home life.

VISION OF THE FUTURE

Having made this 'statement of intent' to yourself, you can now start the process of determining what your future could incorporate. Consider all the data and insights about yourself, your career to date, and your future objectives. Use these to create a picture of a career you would like to be doing in the future. (See also Direction setting pp. 116–117.)

You may fantasize an ideal job or career, and create for yourself in your mind's eye the perfect situation. It is important to bring into the picture not only what you can do, but also what you want to do. Build a comprehensive picture of the future as you would like it to be.

In order to create this picture remember and reflect on all the previous exercises in this section. Now begin to draw some conclusions. Reflect on the information you learned about the environment/role/ circumstances you experienced when you were feeling really satisfied. Remember the people and the type of relationship that

existed and the skills and knowledge you used.

Then think about what you would like and dislike in your work now, your preferences in the type of work you do, how you work, and the context in which you work. Now consider the skills and abilities you have and your major goal or your mission in life.

PETER'S INTERPRETATION

The insights you gain from the exercises you have already completed are very personal. Clearly there is no one right method for completing your vision of the future. However, for those who have difficulty pulling it all together, consider how Peter dealt with his situation and organized all the data he has gathered.

Peter was very satisfied and felt more fulfilled when the following existed:

Environment
● Rural, close to the countryside, in a quiet atmosphere.

Circumstances
● Some travel, but not lengthy commuting. He preferred flexible hours and could work within the pressure of targets and deadlines, but these needed to be self-determined and not totally dependent upon others for their achievement.

Relationships/role/responsibilities
● Peter enjoyed support from his colleagues, and yet was not happy waiting for their input or initiative to the detriment of his own priorities.

On reflection, Peter decided he did not like being a small cog in a big wheel. He was happier when, having gathered sufficient knowledge about the task, working on his own. He could work in a team, but only when the other team members 'lived' up to his own ideas of well defined structure, when his priorities were the same as theirs, and when a peer group operated.

Clearly Peter realized that given the hierarchy of his present company his expectations were a little unrealistic. Indeed, he admitted to himself that he liked to initiate and, while he could be quite good at taking a leadership role, his style would be one of telling and selling rather than participatory or fully consultive. These reflections led him to consider his skills and abilities.

Technically, in the field of software, Peter was very accomplished. His skills in analysis, finding alternative solutions, planning schedules and formats, were all well developed. He had a high capacity for working long, arduous hours, he was self-reliant and presented himself

well to his clients.

In addition, Peter had the ability to see graphically and pictorially the problems and situations he faced. He used his experiences to fit data into a workable framework for action.

Peter also noticed that his values and assumptions about himself were more easily defined. Family life was very important, and spending more time with the family and enjoying himself were now a high priority. He knew that his dislike of conflict had increased, and he tended to walk away rather than confront those who frustrated him.

He wanted to be a useful member of society and the community, and also liked to be recognized and respected for his ideas and technical experience. His two main goals in life seemed to him to be to build a secure home for his family and to make a name for himself.

Peter's choices
Having taken everything into consideration Peter realized he had three choices to make regarding his career. He could either:

● Find another company which specialized in software systems, or one that had a specific data systems department. This would create financial burdens, and there was no guarantee he could make a name for himself.
● Second, he could try to renegotiate his position with his existing company. He had investigated this option and realized it was not feasible.
● Third, he could start his own company designing technical manuals and software packages. This option excited his need to initiate, face a challenge and feel fully involved in something all his own creation. Of course there were risks in this option too, primarily financial, but on balance he decided this was the option he would investigate further.

Peter's vision of the future had some substance which he could now work toward. It may seem fairly radical, but your own vision may involve action just as far-reaching. Each person will have their own view of the future and what it means.

Clearly every vision needs a strategy and direction. Having developed this vision of how you would like your long-term future to look, you must now develop short-term targets and a strategy for achieving them.

This will encourage you to do something positive, and help you maintain a realistic approach to your endeavours. If you do nothing, your long-term goal may seem almost impossible.

DEVELOPING SHORT-TERM TARGETS

Suppose you have decided that you will run your own leisure centre in the future. Your short-term goals might include completing a business management course, finding employment at a local leisure centre and investing a certain sum of money ready to mature at the time you need a lump sum.

All of these goals have certain requirements and time frames. But you will not succeed if you set yourself an impossible task, or make your deadlines so far ahead that progress is unduly slow. Check through your goals and plans with a friend who could give you an objective perspective regarding their feasibility.

You must also consider any barriers that might crop up along the way which could frustrate your achievements. In the example above, this could be the need to attend a basic foundation course prior to registering on a management course. Build in some flexibility, and be prepared to adjust your plans as you progress.

When developing your short-term targets, include in your plans the following people, and list how you are going to involve them.
● Those who can help further develop your action plans.
● Those who can influence the outcome of your plans.
● Those who will be influenced by some of your actions.

PLAN OF ACTION

Deadline date

My long-term goal is		
First short-term goal is		

Requirements/resources	Action necessary	Comments	
1 Skills/knowledge required			
2 Skills/knowledge available			
3 Financial resources needed			
4 Support/involvement of others needed			
5			
6			

ACHIEVING YOUR GOALS

In order to convert these short-term targets into a workable strategy, make sure you look at all the various options that might be available to you. All your short-term goals need to have a time frame set upon them and action steps identified in order to reach them.

For example, your 'overall life mission' may be to make a name for yourself – you envision your future as an influential figurehead within an organization. You will need to determine the options open to you and the information you will need to collect.

To evaluate what movements within your career are necessary for the success of your plan, determine if they should be:

● Vertical, to increase your role within the hierarchy of an organization. Is a large or small organization best suited to you?

● Radial, to increase your importance within an organization. Find out which functions are 'high profile' and critical to a typical organization in your sector of the market.

● Circumferentially, or moving from one function to another to become a leading generalist. Are generalists or specialists usually in positions of leadership within your sector of the market or your organization?

Production

Marketing Sales

Production

Marketing Sales

CONSIDER THE MARKET

You will also need to determine the nature of the labour market and the organizational characteristics of your company.

Labour market characteristics
Consider:
● The demand for labour.
● Any changes in demand.
● If there are seasonal fluctuations.
● The ease of movement between fields.

● If age and experience are prerequisites.

Organizational characteristics
Consider:
● If the company is static or growing.
● The type of structure it has.
● The environment, culture and philosophy of the company.
● The span and limits of jobs.
● The relationships of jobs to each other.

Working through this will help check whether the career movements you desire could conceivably be made within your present organization or, if you would need to move, the type of move you may need to make. It will also make clear whether the criteria you considered in the vision of your future can be incorporated sufficiently well.

★ REMEMBER!

Whatever you want your future working life to be, it is important to consider the example and force yourself to carry out a similar investigatory check.

There are often a number of options available, but you need to look for them before you get down to the actual action planning.

Once you have determined what changes are required, you will need to establish who can help you achieve your goal. This may include people that you already know and work with, or it may be strangers to you who work in your field.

You should not be afraid to make use of the wide variety of resources that is available. These include professional organizations, resource libraries, consultants, books and magazines. The more information you have about what is required for your new job, the more effective your evaluations and assessments can be.

FAMILY AND FRIENDS

People who already know you well can clearly figure in your deliberations. Ask your family what they think of your interpretations when you have worked through the exercises. They may be able to provide you with insights you had not considered.

Elicit their support for your decisions. In many cases, the choice you make will also affect your family. It may be that you will need to take less money, or move house; ask how they feel about these changes.

Your family and friends will be able to provide added dimensions and perspectives on your options and also enlighten you about some of your abilities and aims.

MENTORS

A mentor is someone who you trust who is experienced in your field. Mentors are advisors who help to guide you through the maze of your career. Most mentors are older and more established than the person they are guiding. They are similar to sponsors, although their role is not usually as formalized. Because mentors will have already reached a certain level of success, they will be able to provide you with insights.

You may find a mentor within your immediate workplace; it may be a superior who sees your potential and wants to help you develop it. You may also find mentors outside your workplace, often a tutor or university professor you had a rapport with.

CONSULTANTS

Often called management consultants, personnel consultants or headhunters, these are professional job finders. Most headhunters and consultants deal in the more senior level positions. They are usually hired by the company involved to find the ideal candidate for a job vacancy.

Most fields have consultants who specialize in one particular type of work; for example, finance, education or medicine. Consultants are willing to see job seekers, even if there is no specific job available; they keep many names and numbers on their books. They will also be able to advise you on what jobs are available, what qualifications or experience is needed, what the salaries are and possibly a little about what the different companies are like. Some will help you with your CV or résumé, and help you sell yourself to companies.

JOB EXPERIENCE

If you are unsure about the direction you want to take, you may find it helpful to get some experience before making a full-time commitment. You could test the waters by taking a part-time job or volunteering, if necessary, to gain experience in the profession.

Job experience will allow you to learn more about a field and what is needed to get a job. It can help to answer some of the questions you might have if you are entering a new field.

PROFESSIONAL SOURCES

There are a number of other sources you can use to find out information about your chosen field. These include publications such as magazines and trade journals, professional organizations and even libraries.

Publications will be one of the greatest sources of helpful information. Find out the trade papers and journals that are specific to your field and read them regularly. They can tell you a lot about what is happening in your area.

Most will list job vacancies, providing an indication of what companies are hiring and where areas of growth are. The job vacancies will tell you a lot about the terminology such as job titles, the type of skills and experience needed for a specific job, and what the salaries are that are on offer.

Most areas of employment have professional organizations. Find out which ones are relevant and join, even if you have not entered the field. You will be able to make contacts, meet other people already doing the work you hope to do, and learn more about what is required. Many also offer classes to teach their members advanced skills, and these may be of use to you.

If you need additional advice, contact your local careers service centre. This can provide information about what government schemes are available for retraining or help you if you are setting up your own business.

There are also a number of professional bodies designed specifically to assist with career guidance. Some help to find employment, others give advice on career choices. Most colleges and universities will be able to offer some advice, and to let you know what kind of higher education may be needed. See pp 161–162 for specific addresses.

Living and learning involve a series of seven essential personal capacities or functions. These include will, imagination, thinking, feeling, intuition, sensation and memory.

It is usually assumed that people will develop these various capacities by study-ing school subjects. Or it may be assumed in adulthood that you can or cannot function effectively in these areas. But it is becoming increasingly clear that most people can develop and increase these capabilities if they really want to.

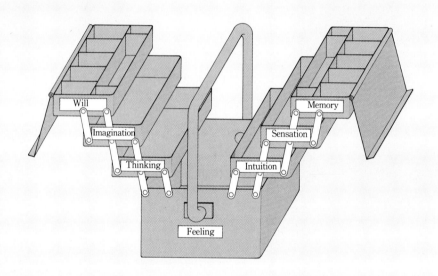

WILL IT BE DIFFICULT?

Developing your capabilities is made slightly more difficult by the fact that they are internal functions of body and mind. They are often intertwined in a complex fashion that makes adequate discrimination of one capability from another almost impossible.

This type of discrimination seems to be necessary for the development of your abilities, just as the parts of a complex skill such as driving a car have to be separated out in order to teach it. Like learning to drive, once you have learned each component, such as braking, steering and using the clutch, you then have to integrate them so that driving becomes semi-automatic. The same applies to the seven basic ways of functioning.

These seven capacities are your psychological toolkit for acting and developing in the world. Everyone is likely to have some of these functions developed but few people will have attained full strength in all of them.

Yet you need a significant degree of competence in each one if you are to become an educated, autonomous and interdependent person.

★ REMEMBER!

You already have a great deal of strength in some of these areas but you may not know it.

It is worth taking the time to identify these strengths. You can then build upon them as your need and motivation energizes you.

WHY DEVELOP CAPABILITIES?

Developing your will can help you take greater charge of your life, or enable you to surrender to your transpersonal will or the will of God in an appropriate way.

Enhancing your imaginative capacity brings rewards in many areas. It can improve your creativity, your memory and your thinking. And it can help open channels to the inner world of archetype and myth which have the potential to re-energize you and unfold the meaning of your life.

Four primary functions
The four functions of thinking, feeling, sensation and intuition, as described by the psychoanalyst Carl Jung, can help you to understand your way of relating to people and the world, which is known as your primary orientation.

Thinking and feeling are concerned with the way you judge the world. Do you judge it from a rational objective or a subjective, emotion-based standpoint?

Sensation and intuition are your ways of perceiving or gathering information from the world. It could be that you perceive information through your five senses (sensation) or through knowing or having a hunch (intuition).

Most people find that they seem to have one of the four functions as a strength and the other as a weak, or undifferentiated,

function. For example, if you are strong on thinking you are probably weak on feeling, while being strong on sensation usually indicates weak intuition.

Jung also coined the terms 'introvert' and 'extrovert' to describe people oriented toward the inner (introvert) or external (extrovert) world. If you are to achieve self-realization, or individuation as Jung calls it, you must develop all four functions.

Knowing what your psychological type is, and what your strongest function is, and whether you are introverted or extroverted, can help you understand your way of encountering the world.

It can also help determine the type of work you might excel at. Many employers are currently using a test based on these psychological types when recruiting or assessing for specific jobs.

The importance of memory
A good memory is another function which is high on the employer's list. If your memory fails, such as when remembering names or things you should have done, it can be embarrassing or have dire consequences. It is important to know that good memories exist because people use them.

Poor memories are poor because they do not get used. Memories usually do not fade. However, information which has been entered and stored properly may get crowded out or superseded by new information.

The suggestions given here to help you develop your capabilities should also help you to understand the meaning and importance of each, and help you to get motivated to start improving your skills. If you are working with functions which you have not yet developed, it will require persistence. Take it slowly to ensure you are developing your capabilities correctly.

Think about whether or not you are controlled by fate. Do you believe that your life, your future and what you might be are determined by biological or social factors that you can do little to change?

If your attitude is fatalistic, you need to realize that you *can* make choices within the limits of your life. Ultimately you have the power to transcend or go beyond these limits. In this your will plays a central role.

WHAT IS WILL?

It was once thought that will was simply sheer determination or will power. That meant sticking with something no matter what the difficulties, or learning to dominate certain aspects of your personality by forceful imposition. However, this notion of the will as discipline, control and authority is only partly true.

Many people have little sense of direction. They are beset by internal conflicts and disperse their energy in meaningless or unconstructive ways. They do not coordinate their lives by using their will and let themselves be tossed about by competing urges, desires and demands. So developing your will offers means of harnessing one of your most valuable capacities.

THE ASPECTS OF WILL

Psychologist Robert Assagioli suggests that there are many aspects of will and not just strong will. The skilful will, for instance, can help you carry out your intentions in a way which does not brutally force, alienate or cause unhelpful resistance in yourself or in others. It can combine with other aspects of your personality, such as your drives and emotions.

Developing good will means not letting selfishness or your desires to possess and dominate rule. It entails learning to make choices which serve both your own and the communal interest, and includes learning to empathize with others.

The transpersonal will can enable you to find meaning and purpose in life beyond simply fulfilling personal needs. It can carry you through feelings of futility and loss of direction which you may feel at many stages in your life. The transpersonal will is your way of transcending your personality and being inspired to engender love, altruistic action, beauty, justice and self-realization.

THE QUALITIES OF WILL

You can probably remember times when you failed to make the effort to change something in your life, or refused to state your opinions when you disagreed with someone. And there will undoubtedly have been times when you said something you knew you shouldn't, and later wished that you had kept your mouth shut.

All of these are examples of weak will, which result in varying degrees of disappointment, remorse or lost opportunity.

The following are qualities associated with the developed will:

- Energy, dynamic power, intensity.
- Mastery, control, discipline.
- Concentration, attention, focus.
- Determination, decisiveness, resoluteness, promptness.
- Persistence, endurance, patience.
- Initiative, courage, daring.
- Organization, integration, synthesis.

★ TRY THIS NOW!

Take some time to examine each set of qualities. Then relate them to your own life by remembering incidents in which you displayed the possession or lack of these qualities.

Allow yourself to dwell fully on the consequences. This may help motivate you to begin developing your will.

DEVELOPING THE WILL

Developing the will can be difficult. You need to have will in order to be able to develop it further. However, for a while you can make use of aspects of yourself until your own will is strong and skilful enough to move forward.

When developing your will, engage your desire to please and your desire for praise. You also need to be playful. Do not take the task too seriously or try to force it or your unconscious will become resistant and sabotage your efforts.

Before you begin, get to know your internal community (see Getting Things Done pp. 112–113) and your drives, needs, instincts and how they operate. This will be of immense benefit when you actually carry out the exercises.

THE PHASES OF WILLING

Some people are accomplished in one or more phases of the willing process and not in others. For example, some have clear intentions but do not know how to put them into action. Others are good at deciding priorities but poor at persisting until their intention has been achieved.

There are different sequential stages in the act of willing. They are:
● Clarifying the aim or purpose; assessing its value in the light of your own value system; arousing motivation strong enough to carry through your intention (by needs and values).

● Deliberation. This means weighing up the pros and cons of this aim or intention in the light of other possible aims. Getting your priorities in order.
● Choosing your aim and deciding to discard others (even if only for the moment). Establishing preference builds responsibility.
● Affirmation or renewal of commitment, which entails being willing to commit yourself to the risk involved, generating a kind of psychological voltage or determination.

● Planning the stages, the sequence, the means and methods in the light of constraints, possibilities and available resources.
● Implementation, which requires that the will skilfully monitors, supervises, directs or harmonizes other aspects of your personality (for example, thinking, feeling, action) to achieve the intended aim. They may require dynamic power, gentle persistence, inhibition of drives or endurance.

★ TEST YOURSELF!

Clarify your understanding of each phase of willing. Which stages reflect your strength? Which indicate a need for development in the light of your current experience?

You will gain some idea of how to enhance the various stages of your willing from the above descriptions. The following are some examples of how this might work:
● *If played with the intention of developing the will, golf, table tennis, skating and climbing help develop attention, concentration, mastery of precise physical action, and endurance.*

● *Reading biographies of outstanding personalities with undivided attention can build motivation. This will develop your will through identification with these people and their achievements.*

● *Performing useless actions systematically, for example moving certain objects at the same time each day, will increase the power of your will. The same is true of simple acts of self denial and inhibition of desire. Keep changing the acts every week or so to avoid irritating your unconscious.*

Imagination is the opposite of realism. It is important because it can help you to conceive a world different from the one in which you actually live. It can help to free you from the prison of your restrictive views of how the world is and what is possible.

Without imagination there would never have been great works of art, the theory of relativity, aeroplanes, a moon landing and much more.

WHAT IS IMAGINATION?

Imagination is the ability to evoke or create an image, a process known as imaging. These images may be spontaneous or called up intentionally. They may be reproductive or creative, that is they may be a copy of an existing image or the creation or adaptation of an image by adding new elements.

Everyone imagines spontaneously a great deal of the time. You may have visual, auditory or kinesthetic (action) images. In most people one sort of image production is more developed than another. Intentional creative imaging is usually more difficult than spontaneous and reproductive imaging. It requires training of the will and concentration as well as the imaging process itself.

Imaging is a right-brain activity, that is it is non-logical, nonverbal, nonlinear and not time-based. In the world of imagination things are not always what they seem. It is the world of the possible and the impossible. It is a potent and impressive world which you can harness through learning the language and processes of image and symbols.

Your imagination can also be used to enhance memory. Recent research shows how great athletes spontaneously rehearse their body movements using images. This is found to improve their performances greatly.

It is also possible to develop your range of skill through imaginative dialogue with a master teacher in a fraction of the time it would take without such two-way contact. The speed results partly from the fact that the images are not time-based like logical language. Therefore a great deal can be learned quickly.

These principles are integrated into the discipline known as Accelerated Learning. Its underlying principle is that by improving your capacity to create images you can improve your ability to learn rapidly and more effectively.

IMPROVING YOUR IMAGING

All the uses of imagination obey the rule that imaging precedes and enhances action. The following are some ways of improving your imaging.

Intentional imaging
Look at a simple object for a minute or two. Now close your eyes and try to reproduce the object visually in your mind's eye and hold it there. This is more difficult than you think.

Some people are unable to produce a visual image but may have a kinesthetic/touch re-creation of the object. Some may be able to reproduce the image but not hold it.

The ability to hold the image will develop with practice. Use your strongest 'mode' and build on this. For example, if you have a sense of the touch you can build in the colour. As you become more adept practise this exercise with more complex objects or groups of objects.

Using symbols
Symbols are images or emblems which stand for something else. They are infused with meaning and have the power to influence. As you improve your familiarity with spontaneous imaging, and pay attention to the images which emerge into your awareness, you will notice that some are more potent or striking than others.

Dreams are an example of your spontaneous imaging. Most people have experienced a nightmare or powerful dream which they may or may not have understood but which had a great impact.

Symbols seem to have a driving force and a direction implicit in them which impels people forward. You may or may not be aware of the power of these symbols because they affect you at conscious and unconscious levels. What is beyond question is that they do influence you. It is

possible to harness this energy by consciously responding to spontaneous symbols thrown up by your psyche, and by actively and wisely engaging those symbols which channel the energies which you need.

As you become more familiar with your imaginative processes, and more accustomed to the meaning or nature of the symbols that affect you personally, you will be able to gain access to powerful stores of energy. These can be released and channelled toward helping you achieve your goals.

In using symbols in this way people often seem to experience intense vitality. They also experience a new harmony between their inner selves and their external actions in the world. Techniques of active imagination and the recalling of dreams are ways of engaging your inner world and its symbols.

LEARNING FROM YOUR DREAMS

To learn from your dreams do this exercise, if possible with a friend or group.
● Retell a dream in the first person and present tense as if it is happening now.
● Choose the part that affects you most and become the characters/objects in

the dream. Speak as if you were them. Let them tell you about themselves.
● Becoming each character in turn, conduct a dialogue with the other characters. Notice how they respond, notice any hidden conflicts which emerge and see if

there are any similarities with your life as you experience it. Be willing to act out each character, moving position for each character to gain the most benefits.
● Carry on the dream where it finished and notice what happens next. Does it have any message for you?

Always keep a pen and paper by your bed to record your dreams. Even simply recording your dreams regularly will result in recurring themes and symbols whose significance will gradually make themselves felt.

People who have a well-developed thinking function tend to approach the world in a logical and analytical way. They find it easier to respond to other people's thoughts and do not show emotion very readily.

Thinkers like theories and models and use them to predict outcomes. They are usually objective and impersonal in their decision making. They are good at sorting out what is the 'best' course of action when considering a range of criteria. However, these people may have difficulty deciding whether they like the result or whether they feel happy about it.

WHAT IS THINKING?

Intellectual ability is highly valued in Western culture, and the thinking function has received much attention in educational systems. Yet you may have the impression that you were never taught how to 'think', or perhaps you never quite realized that you were.

Thinking can be described as the revolving of ideas in the mind, for example, examining, reflecting on, linking, being critical of objects, products of your imagination, memories, awareness, insights and so on.

Of course what goes on in the mind is a highly complex business and entails imagination, attention, perception and remembering, as well as thinking.

While these functions all contribute to and complement thinking it is best to treat thinking as separate for the purpose of clarification and development.

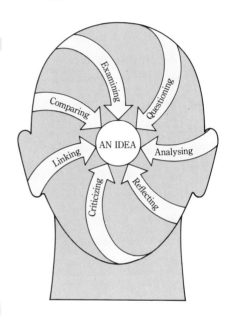

YOUR THINKING FRAMEWORK

Everyone has frameworks which they use in thinking, though they may not be aware of them. Frameworks (theories, models, maps and concepts) are your way of organizing knowledge and experience.

The first time you encounter something or somebody you have an experience which forms the basis of a personal construct or a way of viewing the world.

A construct entails a belief or an understanding of what the world is and how it works. It also embodies an evaluation or emotional judgement about yourself, the world and the relationship between the two.

You then tend to approach, understand and predict events in the world in terms of these constructs. Similarly, most of your constructs change and evolve as you encounter new experiences which you cannot understand in terms of your old constructs. Often these constructs are formed and re-formed intuitively and unconsciously and are not articulated verbally. Thus as you grow older you are capable of greater understanding.

A concept (the cognitive part of the construct) is a general notion of how things work. Concepts, like theories, models and maps, are the tools of the thinker. Their value depends on their capacity to describe, explain or predict, and prediction is more useful in life than description alone.

Descriptive maps or models help recognition. Explanatory maps and models say how and why it is so. Predictive maps and models indicate what is likely to occur given certain conditions and in particular contexts. These predictions enable you to plan and prepare for events and experiences so that you can gain the most advantage when they occur.

THE BASIC SKILLS

Good thinkers consciously use a wide range of maps, models, concepts and theories which they can apply to their area of interest. Many of these theories are evolved or used within the various subject disciplines studied at school or college, such as mathematical models, geographical maps, theories of gravity, stages of embryo development or the concept of pressure.

Most of these disciplines have developed a variety of specialized means of thinking. While you may not need such specialist languages for thinking you do need a language, you need some theoretical and experiential knowledge of your subject, and you need some basic thinking skills.

Definition
To state the exact meaning of the words you use. Do not assume you have the same experience in mind as someone else when you use a word.

Suspension of belief
To discover a new construct or concept you have to temporarily disbelieve the old one and endure some confusion before the new one emerges.

Asking questions and formulating problems
Effective thinking often depends most on asking the right questions or formulating a problem in a way that makes it easier to solve.

Brainstorming
Noting down what you already know. Judgement or evaluation come later.

Categorizing and prioritizing
These can help bring order and a degree of clarity by sorting data.

Analysing
This usually occurs within some existing framework or theory, for example, to discriminate between facts and assumptions. Analysis also helps break information down into its elements and exposes underlying relationships and organizational principles.

Inferring
What is unstated but can be deduced or implied from given information.

Comparing and contrasting
Examining similarities, differences, pros and cons of two or more propositions, products or events. Comparing and contrasting is a useful exercise in decision making.

Hypothesizing and falsifying
Creating or inventing a theory, or a way of predicting or explaining, and attempting to prove it incorrect with argument and evidence. A hypothesis is assumed true until proven false.

Particularizing or generalizing
This is performed to predict outcomes on the basis of evidence.

Devil's advocate
Taking a variety of hypothetical perspectives to rattle and shake a notion or examine it critically.

Problem-solving cycles
Moving sequentially, to test out your theory, from causes to effects, to possible solutions to chosen solutions.

People whose strength lies in the emotional domain usually make judgements based on their personal likes and dislikes – their gut reaction. They are clear about how they feel and are sensitive to the feelings of others. They are often oriented toward past memories, warmth and harmony, and meaningful relationships are important to them.

Their own values and associations, and the values and associations of others, feature large in their decisions. Their intensity of feeling can lead to moodiness, but they usually have a highly developed capacity for bonding and relating to most people.

WHAT ARE EMOTIONS?

Basically, emotions are subtle discriminations of the pleasure-pain response. It has been suggested that anger is a response to blocked choice, fear to blocked understanding and grief to blocked love. For example our basic human needs are connected dynamically to our emotional states. Joy, delight, exuberance and ecstasy are aspects of the pleasure response.

You have a number of healthy options for managing your emotions, though the first option is the one most people use. You can:

● Express them verbally and/or with full physical motion, such as crying, shaking or storming.

● Control them by no longer identifying with them, by repressing or suppressing them.

● Release them cathartically in a non-destructive manner and in an appropriate place.

● Transmute or transform them into constructive action, artistic creation, or self-realization.

People who are emotionally literate are:
● Aware of their bodily response to events or people.
● Able to discriminate between one type of response and another.

● Able to identify various physiological responses with appropriate emotional labels.
● Able to choose the most effective ways of acting and are not controlled by their emotions.

● Able to recognize and limit the effects of past distress and its restimulation in everyday life.
● Can accept and value their positive and negative feelings.
● Take responsibility for their feelings.

They do not blame others for making them feel the way they do.
● Equipped with a range of options for managing their emotions, for example, expression, control and catharsis.

DISCOVERING YOUR EMOTIONS

Often it is hard for people to recognize their feelings, particularly negative feelings. Discrimination of feelings needs to be acquired or learned. You need to have your feelings accepted and valued before you can learn such discrimination.

You often receive messages from those around you which tell you that your emotions are childish or shameful. The response to the expression of emotion is one of alarm or embarrassment rather than respect and acceptance.

To avoid such censure and reaction you may tend to hide strong emotions under a veil of more acceptable emotions, for example boredom, embarrassment or tension.

When you search a little deeper, by using techniques such as non-stop talking, laughter and physical stretching and yawning, you encounter the stronger primary emotions such as anger, fear, grief, happiness and joy.

What are your choices?

You have a number of choices of behaviour when you wish to express your emotions. First, you need to notice your physiological response and label it. The sensitive person may well have noticed what emotion you are feeling from your nonverbal expression but remember, you do not have to verbalize your emotion or act on it in some other way when you become aware of it.

A second option follows from the first. You can verbalize the emotion by choosing the appropriate word to help the receiver understand the true extent of the emotion you are experiencing. For example, if you are angry you might say you are annoyed, irritated or in a murderous rage. If you feel fear, you may say you feel anxious or terror. Grief may be expressed by disappointment or despair.

This variation in intensity tells you how important one thing is in relation to another, or defines your priorities. You often need to communicate using various intensities of expression to let others know how important something is to you. Otherwise, the person may misconstrue your meaning if you do not create the appropriate emphasis.

A third option is to give full nondestructive expression to your feelings, including the verbal aspect. For example, expression of anger might include storming, shouting and excitement, and may include physical gestures such as jumping up and down and issuing shouts of excitement. Similarly fear may include trembling or screaming.

Many people will find this level of expression difficult to realize and uncomfortable to experience. Our culture represses this type of expression through its implicit and often explicit inhibition. Thus you may have to relearn how to express your feelings.

If this is the case you will need to relearn bodily expressiveness or at least to stop blocking it. By educating or re-educating your expressive capacities you are more likely to skilfully and appropriately express your emotions as the need arises. The cathartic approach is best for this purpose.

It is also probably true to say that your deepest feelings transcend the personal and are experienced more as bliss, oneness, ecstasy, lack of boundaries, or a peak. Many people experience such joys only periodically.

You are more likely to have sustained feelings such as these as you realize more of your own potential. As you enter these states of peak experience words seem to be less relevant and necessary.

★ REMEMBER!

Your emotions, when functioning well, can:
- *Help you find out what you want and what is right for you.*

- *Tell you something needs changing in you, in others and in the world.*
- *Help communicate your priorities and needs to others.*

- *Help you empathize with others and with yourself.*
- *Warn you of danger.*

- *Motivate you to grow.*
- *Help you clarify your own values and guide you.*

Intuition is useful for seeing the potential, possibility or emergent direction in situations. It enables you to find out about relations and meanings beyond sensory data.

People with a highly developed intuition can be visionaries, entrepreneurs, inventors and artists because of their interest in what they might become and in what the future holds in store.

Intuitors are unconventional and follow their own inspiration, reach conclusions quickly and are impatient with routine. Precision takes time, so they often make errors of fact. They like solving problems, learning new skills and work in enthusiastic bursts of energy. They have a knack of tuning in to undercurrents of what is hidden, and have insights or hunches which are often reached at an unconscious level.

WHAT IS INTUITION?

Intuition is a holistic awareness or a direct knowing of something. In it, a person appears to bring past experience, present knowledge, imagination and the external environment together in a way which gives rise to the insight or intuition. Intuition is not an act of wilful control, but an attentive state of receptivity.

For some, being intuitive may mean stopping the internal noise of their thinking and creating an opening for an image or kinesthetic sense. For most it will entail a blurring of contact or a defocusing on the sensory aspects of external reality.

Your intuition may be a clear unerring insight. At other times it may be completely off the mark. Intuitions must be checked against experience. Having an intuition and being able to articulate or interpret it in a useful manner are separate skills. You cannot control your intuition, and the more you force it the less available to you it will become.

THE IMPORTANCE OF INTUITION

It is an observable fact that Western culture does not value the intuitive function as much as it does the rational function, on which it often depends for inspiration. The education system does not encourage its development either directly or indirectly, yet intuitive functioning is in great demand.

Whether it is through lack of education, or the very nature of intuition, it is difficult to elucidate what your intuitor does. Clearly, if you are to develop your intuition you need to do so with clear intention and believe that it is possible to acquire knowledge other than through sensory perception or book learning.

Be open to receive intuitions. You need to slow down internally and attend to images, verbalized thoughts, feelings and sensations which occur within in response to the situation in a state of 'unattached witnessing'.

AWAKENING INTUITION

The following have been found useful in awakening intuition.

Relaxation
This is essential for the development of intuition, though once developed intuition can occur at any time. You can relax by sequentially tensing each individual part of your body and letting it go again. It may help to state the following: 'I'm relaxing my scalp, my scalp is relaxing' for each part.

Meditation
This can help promote inner silence and quiet the mind. It can be an open focus or an attempt to clear the mind by imaginatively expanding the space between various organs.

Or, it might be a focus exercise to aid concentration, for example by being aware of your breathing and drawing your attention back when it wanders. These exercises require persistence.

KEYS TO DEVELOPING INTUITION

There are a number of practices that can stabilize and validate your intuitions. They will also help you to allow yourself to learn to trust your intuitions and enable you to check out their validity with other people. The keys to developing your intuition include:

● Be nonjudgemental. This is at the heart of good perception.

You will need to learn self-acceptance and acceptance of people and things as they are, rather than trying to push them to what they should be.

● Be open. If you are afraid of being seen you may close up and be unable to see.

● Identify with another person, for example through emotional empathy. Identification is a

vital element of intuition. This ability is facilitated by love and compassion and hindered by self-deception and projection (seeing as belonging to someone else something that is really part of yourself).

● Have a support group with whom you can share your intuition and intuitive explorations. Being a member of such a

group can accelerate the process of development.

● Practise exercises daily and keep a journal of intuitive flashes.

● Explore the language of images and symbols, which are often the most potent vehicle for conveying your intuitions into consciousness. This is best done in a support group.

CLEARING A SPACE

To allow your intuition to function you have to get out of your own way, so to speak. That is, you need to stop the hyperactivity which is usually going on in your head. The following exercise is one process for clearing your mental space to allow your intuition to come through.

● First, find a quiet place to sit.

● Close your eyes, take some deep breaths and relax.

● Ask yourself what is stopping you from being content right now.

● Allow a verbal answer or an image to emerge.

● Welcome and accept this answer but do not get involved in solving or investigating the problem or the worry.

● Let the problem go by visualizing that you are putting it in a box in a safe place,

burying it, tying it to a floating balloon or dropping it into a lake. Any number of images can be used for this. Choose the one you feel most comfortable with.

● When you have let the problem go, repeat the process by asking the question again. Continue doing this until you have a clear space in your mind.

● Your ability to clear a space will improve with practice.

People who have well developed senses excel at gathering hard facts using their eyes, ears and other sense organs. They are realists, with their feet firmly planted on the ground, and attend to specifics and concrete data in the here and now. They like standard procedures and routines. They are not particularly inspired, but seldom make errors of fact and tend to be good at precise and specific work.

They are patient with detail and can be impatient with complexity. Although they may not have an overview they will persist through to the conclusion of projects. They like moving into action – sometimes before plans are complete.

WHAT IS SENSORY FUNCTION?

Sensory experience is critical to the development of meaning. In many schools experience-based learning has re-emerged to complement abstract book learning. As a result of book learning and the status given to it, many people often assume they know the meaning or experiential basis of the words they use.

Often you have limited sensory experience, usually visual, because you have little opportunity for hands on experience. This can lead to misunderstanding and poor communication. Often, too, you trust what you are told rather than taking the trouble to see for yourself.

Sensory experience takes time. Most city dwellers are too busy looking for answers or going places to savour their sensory experiences. Artists, scientists, poets and cooks know the importance of deepening the quality of their sensory capacities. Their very livelihood and excellence is based on acute abilities to observe, taste, touch, listen and smell.

While we live in a culture which places a high value on the sciences we also live in a culture in which the work ethic prevails, a culture short on pleasure and long on pain. As a result, many people spend a great deal of time trying to control and dominate the world and too little time enjoying it. You may find you spend much time making lists of what you have to do and little time listing those things which give you pleasure.

Pleasure and vitality are infectious. If you are in touch with your own delight and pleasure it rubs off on those around you, usually with positive results. Problems shrink and difficult people do not seem so difficult when you are in a state of pleasure.

WAYS TO AWAKEN THE SENSES

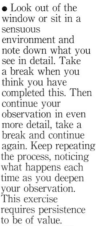

There is fairly clear evidence that the quality of your sensory experience plays a major part in your ability to memorize and in the development of your intelligence. The quality as well as the quantity of sensory data you receive is a key factor to using your senses to solve your problems.

Few would argue against the necessity or desirability of sensory acuity, yet most do little to improve it in adult life. You can and must if you wish to deepen this capacity.

The following exercises are ways in which you can awaken and develop your senses.

● Observe a group of people in a public place and record it. When you have done this see if you can separate out your thoughts, feelings and imaginings from the sensory data. How much of what you recorded came from your senses? What does this tell you about your use of your five senses? Do this exercise with a friend and compare notes.

● List your own pleasures and delights. Choose one and allow yourself time to re-experience it. What senses have you allowed to give you pleasure?

● Look out of the window or sit in a sensuous environment and note down what you see in detail. Take a break when you think you have completed this. Then continue your observation in even more detail, take a break and continue again. Keep repeating the process, noticing what happens each time as you deepen your observation. This exercise requires persistence to be of value.

● Take time with a partner to surprise each other with sensory delights, ranging across all five senses. This could be tasting delicious foods, listening to relaxing music or smelling subtle perfumes. Notice the difference between the feelings before and after you have experienced this. Notice how it affects your next activity.

● Put on a blindfold or close your eyes. In a familar place, or a room full of people carrying out a similar exploration or a walled garden, allow yourself to explore the contents through touch, taste and smell. Notice the differences from your usual way of exploring. What is the difference in information, quality and impact of this kind of sensory contact?

At some time or another, you will have been required to learn by heart, memorize or learn by rote. Possibly you came away from this believing that you had a dreadful memory. No learning takes place without memory, so you may also have decided that you were a poor learner and perhaps of low intelligence.

This is a sad state of affairs, and an unnecessary one. You may think you have a poor memory. In fact, you appear to store every detail of your experience but it may be that you do not know how to gain access to it or recall it.

WHAT MAKES A GOOD MEMORY?

Those who do have good memories have been found to be consistent and regular users of their memory. Thus they retain skills which would otherwise atrophy from lack of use.

For example, good memorizers have excellent ways of entering information into their memory systems, good ways of retaining it and efficient means of getting it out again when necessary. Good memory depends on such skills. It also depends on a variety of other factors which you need to be aware of.

Values and needs
Two questions might help clarify your motivation to remember. Ask yourself what you want to remember it for? And how badly do you need to remember it? The more potent your value and need the more you will remember.

Self-image and personality type
If you believe you are worthwhile as a person, that your memory is good, and that you can remember, you are already on the way to success. Different personality types tend to remember different things.

For example, intuitors remember ideas, sensors details of fact, feeling types what goes on in a relationship. What is your tendency? You can also improve your memory for other types of information by improving these functions.

Meaning and relevance
People remember what they understand, that is, what fits into their existing overview through linking and associations. Personal involvement with the material will lead to stronger memories. Familiarity with the area means you know where to anchor your new information.

Stance and readiness
Generally, the more open to or prepared you are for new information the more likely you are to remember it. You often tend to neutralize, distort or forget the information which poses a threat to you. Relaxing and choosing a secure and familiar environment helps to minimize your defences and prejudicial attitudes.

The beginning, middle and ending
When you have to remember a great deal of information it is best to break up the input where possible. This is because you tend to remember the first and last things you hear and often forget the middle part. Cut the middle short by taking breaks.

Impact and attention
You remember most of those events or objects to which you have given the most attention and/or which have had the most impact. That is, those which have been outstanding from an emotional, revelatory, or sensational point of view.

If you are trying to remember something specific, giving it your undivided or free attention is most productive.

The power of imagination
The creation of strong images is central to memory storage or retention. You remember easily what is most memorable, active, exciting, distinctive or moving. Your imagination has the power to make memorable even the most trivial. You can learn to use the power of imagination when improving your memory.

IMPROVING YOUR MEMORY

Good memorizing takes time. Most people are often so rushed that they do not allocate the time to remember. However, you often have to repeat something to remember it. This can waste more time because repetition on its own is a poor way of trying to remember.

Give your memory a chance to learn. This will be slow at first, because you may be learning to remember as well as trying to remember. Like a computer, you have a short-term memory and a long-term memory. Your short-term capacity is what you can remember in about 15 seconds, while long-term memory is the storage which is not linear, historical or time limited.

Short-term memory could be described as the active or working part of your memory. For a longer-lasting effect you must convert short-term memory to storage. This is where good technique is necessary. The following are a few helpful techniques.

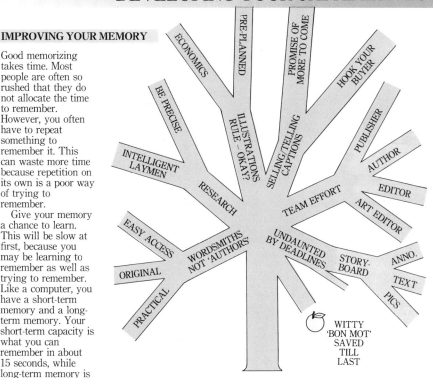

Encoding
To remember names, watch the person's face while you internally create a striking image which makes the name memorable. Say the name while visualizing the image.

You can remember lists by connecting numbers with rhyming words and visualizing an imaginative interaction between the rhyming words and the points to be remembered, and expect total recall.

Try it out with a list of things formulated as key words. You want to use visualization to create an imaginative link between the rhyming word and the key word.

You can also:
● Link or deposit information to or in memorable localities.
● Write down, draw, dance, visualize, as well as verbalize.
● Categorize, lump together, understand underlying organizing principles.
● Create a story integrating points to remember.

Retaining
Learn and recall, then later recall and learn. You can ensure storage by using this sequence for a short time in repeated sessions rather than trying to remember information all at once.

Recall
● Flash imaging involves catching quick images rather than pushing or labouring the remembering.
● Association is letting one image spark off the next.
● Literal description is describing the sensory or concrete aspects of a subject in detail (even if it is peripheral to what you are trying to remember), filling in details you cannot recall in the way you imagine they would have been. This will tend to evoke the abstract details.
● Mind maps involve writing out memories as key words. These are not arranged in linear form, but as associative diagrams with one idea linking to the next around a central topic.

Managing yourself effectively means knowing what the job is about. At its simplest the job of self-management might be described as meeting all your needs, including your desire to be in harmonious and supportive relationships with others and with your environment.

The American psychologist Abraham Maslow outlined a map of needs based on his study of a range of successful people from many walks of life. These people he called self-actualizers, and they were probably also effective self-managers.

INDIVIDUAL ACTIVITIES

The task of the individual might be described as self-actualization. It is becoming who you really are, realizing your unique capabilities and achieving meaningful goals. Self-actualization gives depth, meaning and direction to your life.

Effective self-management means harnessing what happens internally within you, and your actions in the external social world, to the goal of self-realization. Such harnessing means that you are more likely to choose behaviours that meet your own needs and, at the same time, serve the needs of society, though this may not always be apparent.

Some people behave in ways that are likely to lead to self-actualization while others are more concerned with surviving. Part of the reason for this is that people need to be competent at meeting the lower needs in the hierarchy scale (see chart) before attending to the higher ones. Usually once the lower needs can be met successfully the higher ones emerge and can then be dealt with.

However, meeting of the basic needs is no guarantee that you would automatically move on to attend to your needs for growth. There are a number of reasons why you might not move into self-actualizing behaviours.

These include being locked into unproductive behaviours (habits) from the past, group pressure against self-actualizing behaviour and inner defences, such as pretence and dishonesty, which keep you out of touch with yourself.

WHAT ARE THE BASIC NEEDS?

Your basic needs are as follows.
● Physiological needs, such as food, sleep, water and warmth.
● Safety and security, including freedom from fear and violence, shelter, order and stability.
● Belonging and love, for example in friendship, having a place in a group or family, social approval and acceptance.
● Esteem, including self-respect, status, mastery of a skill, being valued by others and independence.

When you were a child these needs were met in various ways. During childhood you may have been helped to develop self-actualizing behaviours. For example, efficient perception of reality, acceptance of self and others, spontaneity and having a problem-solving attitude toward life.

However, not everyone will have been lucky enough to have had a supportive caring environment. But whatever your childhood, as an adult you are expected to be responsible for meeting those needs yourself.

The lower the need on the hierarchy the more powerful and immediate is its demand for fulfilment. The higher needs require adequate management of the lower needs on the hierarchy before they are likely to receive significant attention. They are more delicate but they may also override the lower needs on occasions.

These lower needs give way to the more potent needs when survival becomes an issue. For example, playfulness and curiosity are self-actualizing behaviours which noticeably, even in childhood, disappear when we are hungry or are under threat.

Meta needs are those archetypal or spiritually motivated needs which seem to transcend the personal, for example pursuit of justice, faith and peace. Knowledge and freedom are continual needs which seem to be felt at all levels of the hierarchy.

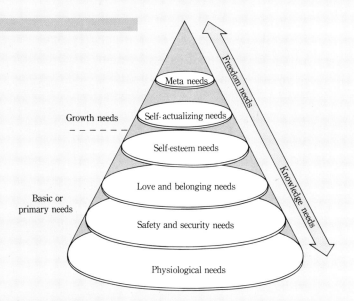

Meta needs

Self-actualizing needs

Self-esteem needs

Love and belonging needs

Safety and security needs

Physiological needs

Growth needs

Basic or primary needs

Freedom needs

Knowledge needs

WHAT ARE YOU TRYING TO ACHIEVE?

Whether or not you agree with the purpose of life outlined by Maslow you will need to clarify what it is that you are trying to achieve. Otherwise you will end up reacting to internal and external pressures in a hopelessly disorganized fashion.

Regardless of who you are you are faced with certain life challenges if you wish to become autonomous and realize some of the potential that lies within you. These challenges are:
● Survival.
● Maintaining your self and your relationships.
● Learning and developing.
● Self transcendence and adventure.

Each of these entails action which requires varying levels of knowledge and skills. This is further complicated by the fact that you keep changing, for instance by getting older or moving home. Equally, your circumstances may be changed by factors beyond your control.

SUCCESSFUL SELF-MANAGEMENT

Self-management means maintaining a sense of balance. For example, balancing action with relaxation, work with home, head with heart and doing with being.

All successful self-management requires courage, flexibility, a sense of direction, self-knowledge and an ability to attend to detail while, at the same time, keeping an overview.

Whether you see the management task as meeting your needs, responding to life challenges or some other purpose, it is essential to have an objective or sense of direction if you are going to manage yourself effectively.

Paradoxically, it is often only when you try to manage others that you realize you are not very good at managing yourself. If you are to manage others it becomes imperative that you also are an effective self-manager.

★ TRY THIS NOW!

Outline various areas in your life, for example, family, work and friends. Decide at what level your self-management is functioning in each, for example survival, maintenance, and transcendence. Also, determine the level of satisfaction you gain. What changes would you like to make?

Managing is often defined as getting things done through others. If you can imagine that you have an internal community or a series of subpersonalities (see Mapping Your Life pp. 12–27) then you will be able to put this notion of getting things done through others into practice.

MANAGING YOUR INTERNAL COMMUNITY

Your internal community contains the 'people' you are going to manage and who will help or hinder you in achieving your goals. The 'you' in this case is the self who witnesses what you are doing and who makes decisions. It is that independent centre of your being who weighs up the options and whose will leads to action.

Your internal community, on the other hand, comprises all those subpersonalities and needs which demand attention and expression. To get to know your internal community, you will need to identify the various social roles that you play.

Determining the characters from art, cinema and literature with whom you identified, or who have had an emotional impact on you, will also help you get to know your internal community.

KNOWING YOUR COMMUNITY

Often your relationship with those who strongly attract or repel you can help you discover some members of your internal community you have not yet got to know. This is because you project on to others parts of yourself you have not yet become aware of or accepted as your own.

If you are going to self-manage effectively it is essential that you get to know your internal community. You may have a destructive saboteur or a creative genius that you did not know about. You may also need to bring in some new members by doing some training or self-development to balance your team.

It is the self-manager's job to maintain an independent stance and not become overidentified with and dominated by any of the internal community. It is the manager's job to ensure that needs of your community can be met and that their particular qualities or talents are used effectively.

This will also mean orchestrating and resolving conflicts to maintain harmony between competing needs. Your will is the channel through which you achieve balance, and it may be worthwhile taking some time to develop it (see Developing Your Capabilities pp. 50–65).

As with all successful management systems the independent manager has to gain the confidence, credibility and cooperation of the team. Autocratic imposition of your will, for example by repressing some of your community and their needs, will result in creating rebels and saboteurs. It will also result in poor follow-through on decisions. A healthy internal community will require balance, fair play and skilful handling if it is to be maintained in working order.

★ TRY THIS NOW!

● *Make a note of any of the roles or characters who influenced you or with whom you can identify.*
● *See if you can get some sense of the purpose, the needs and the qualities (for example assertiveness, love, arrogance, vulnerability) which belong to each.*
● *Do you notice anything about the range and nature of your internal community? For instance, would it comprise a balanced team for getting things done?*
● *Which are active, that is, which are noticeably present in your behaviour in various situations? Who dominates your community overall, and who gets shut out or is just not appreciated?*
● *Are there any you wish were not present? Are there any who do not get on with each other?*

INTEGRATING YOUR COMMUNITY

People often experience an internal split within themselves. This can be either creative or debilitating. It is often as if the parent in us demands that our internal child changes in some way. Your internal child often ignores, avoids, rebels, fearfully complies or even pretends to comply.

The way to progress is to get the two sides to dialogue, honouring each other's position, and finding a compromise which meets both goals or needs, rather than one dominating or sabotaging the other. This process is similar to conflict resolution between real people except that they are internal parts of yourself which you externalize and role play to make the conflict more accessible and manageable.

★ TEST YOURSELF!

Make a list of the all the 'shoulds', 'musts' and 'have to's' that you are aware of and pick one to work with. Place two cushions or chairs opposite each other. Sit in one chair and imagine yourself in the other position. Begin telling yourself how you should be, what you must do, and so on.

When you have finished, sit on the opposite cushion and reply. Notice how you feel in response to what has been said. Express your verbal and nonverbal responses.

Switch back to the 'should' position again and notice how this is different from the other. Notice your body posture, gauge the tone of your voice, etc. Do they remind you of anybody you know? It is certainly an internal stance you take toward yourself.

If you recognize who might have spoken to you in that way, allow the dialogue to continue as if the dialogue is with that person as they were then but in the first person present tense. Say what they might say, using their manner and language. What was their message?

Now become yourself – as you were then – and respond to them. What do you need to say that you have not said? Notice what your needs and attitudes are, for example, you might have needed appreciation.

Speak aloud when working in this way. Remember, it does not matter whether you recognize the person externally or not. These characters are members of your internal community and dialogue is equally relevant.

Maintaining health and vitality is not about diet and exercise. It is about being aware of the wisdom of your own body, the momentum of your emotions, the gymnastics of your mind and wellspring of your soul and your spirit.

Take notice of and learn to interpret the messages your body, mind and emotions are constantly sending you. Doing this, and maintaining a balance between them and your functioning in the world, will set you on the way to health and well-being.

THE WISDOM OF YOUR BODY

Most people have no problem noticing when they are hungry, in pain or sleepy but many have difficulty being aware of all parts of their bodies. Take a moment to give attention to your body. Which parts of your body emerge spontaneously into your awareness and which have you difficulty contacting?

Notice the pressure, movement, energy and tension you feel. Intentionally exaggerate any sensations if you want to bring them more into awareness. What kind of message is this sensation giving you?

HEARTFELT EMOTIONS

Many people in Western culture are taught from an early age to suppress or repress their emotions. For many this long term suppression has meant that they are no longer capable of contacting certain emotions and are unable to express or release them.

Women are most likely to lose touch with their ability to express anger, while men tend to suppress fear or grief.

When such suppression continues it may eventually emerge in the form of physical or mental illness. Learning to release blocked up feelings and recover the ability to express the full range of your emotions will increase your vitality and intelligence. The first stage is learning to recognize your emotions and discriminate between them.

★ TRY THIS NOW!

Pick a symptom, for example a current headache or muscle tension. Give it loving attention, especially if it is painful. Accept it and welcome it into your awareness. Notice which parts of your body are affected and how they are affected. Increase the symptom if you can, and then release it, noticing how you do it. Explore it in detail.

Now become the symptom. Is this symptom what you are like? Describe yourself (as the symptom) and what you do to this person (you). How do you make him feel, and what is your attitude toward him? Now become yourself again and respond to the symptom. What is going on between

you? Become the symptom again. As the symptom are you useful to him?

Take some time to reflect on what you have learned when you have continued the dialogue back and forth for a while and each has said what they would like of the other.

When you have finished, become the symptom again and

converse with the people in your host's (your) life. Tell him how you affect him, what you get him to do, how you do it and so on.

Let the dialogue continue and then reflect on the wisdom of your body or notice how you have silenced it. What could you do to relieve the symptom? If you do not know, ask it.

★ TEST YOURSELF!

Relax on a chair, making sure you are comfortable. Breathe deeply half a dozen times, and let go of your control of your breathing.

Now pay attention to what is going on in your mind. Witness it, but do not try to direct it. Are you getting visual or kinesthetic (action) images, or auditory conversations? Are you attending to the past, the present or the future events? Do you focus on one event or flit from one to the other? What kinds of images do you select and which do you avoid or not attend to, the pleasant or the unpleasant?

Are these patterns of attention and awareness familiar, satisfying, draining or energy giving? What happens if you do the opposite to what you noticed? What have you learned about how your mind works which can help you maintain your health and vitality?

MENTAL GYMNASTICS

Many people are prisoners in their minds. They are like pressurized bottles tightly corked and everything gets pushed in there. Is it any wonder that they turn to alcohol, drugs or numerous other ways to relieve the pressure?

It has been suggested that people use only 10 per cent of their mental capacity. And even that small amount is used poorly, causing unnecessary mental stress. Take some time to notice how your mind works to take some of the pressure off.

★ TRY THIS NOW!

Bring to mind an incident involving someone you are angry or have been angry with. Evoke the details of the event, describe it literally to yourself, visualize it and experience the feeling of anger fully. Notice the bodily sensations that go with it.

What is happening, for example with your arms, your neck and shoulder muscles, your eyes, your breathing, posture and pulse? Now notice what you did with your anger and all the accompanying symptoms and words? Is this a familiar pattern? How do you feel now? Are you satisfied or do you feel you need to change?

Repeat the exercise for different emotions, such as fear, grief, happiness, boredom or embarrassment to get an overview of how you manage your emotions.

THE WELLSPRING OF THE SOUL

Soul and spirit provide means of describing the transpersonal elements of your being, or those inner sources from which you draw deeper meaning, relevance and inspiration in your life. They are how you contact the divine in yourself and others.

Religion has lost its significance for many people today. Some would see this as the cause of much of the meaninglessness, inner despair and loss of vision apparent in Western society today.

The archetypal and transpersonal psychologies can provide an alternative outlet for discovering and developing your higher self. But even those who reject traditional religion must recognize that the spiritual or soulful dimension is necessary to maintain health and realize your full potential.

A number of different methods are available for getting in touch with your spirit or soul. Many people have found the following to be valuable.
● Retreats from external distractions to attend and listen to the quiet depth of your being.
● Meditation or prayer.
● Aesthetic experiences of art, music, nature.
● Religion, ritual, ceremony.
● Symbolic work with dreams and active imagination.

Many people experience considerable stress because they see themselves as being unable to fit all they 'have' to do into the available time. Others spend their time doing things they do not value highly or cannot see the relevance of.

Busy people need to budget their time in the way that most people have to budget money. Remember, everybody has exactly the same amount of time. The key to having time is choosing how to use it.

SELF-MANAGEMENT AND TIME

Time is irreversible and irreplaceable. To waste your time is to waste your life. If you value your time so will others. If you do not why should they. Do you value yourself and your time?

Time management is just part of self-management, and it is as much an attitude and philosophy of life as a mechanical exercise in clock watching.

If you have not bothered to sort out your values, priorities and what your life is

ORGANIZING YOUR TIME

The following methods of time management are meant to help you achieve more control over your life and enable you to function more efficiently and effectively. They can also be used to make your life more stressful by compulsively stuffing more and more into each day. Think quality not quantity in your life and strive for balance, not obsession.

Key areas
These are the main areas in your life, the ones in which you have responsibilities and must produce results. What is entailed in these areas may be explicit, as in the case of a job description, or implicit or unclear as in family responsibilities.

It is important to clarify your reason for being by answering the question: 'For what purpose am I here?'

Check the answer with those concerned to ensure agreement. Draw a pie chart representing the distribution of your time by dividing the circle proportionally.

Then check the balance of the time you spend against your goals, values and priorities. If you are not spending your time on the areas you feel are important, set about renegotiating the way you spend your time.

Priorities
Some people prioritize aspects of their life into 'must do' and 'should do', with 'want to do' coming a disappointing third. This method seems to be based on other people's priorities. Make sure the priorities you use are yours.

Use this method, for example, for the week ahead. Identify those tasks which:
● Could be scheduled (proactive tasks).
● Crop up unscheduled (reactive tasks).

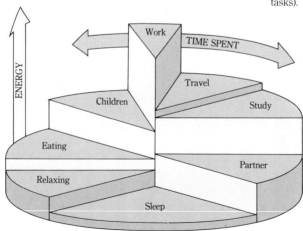

about, then all the wonderful techniques will not make life less stressful or more satisfying.

Exercising choice requires that you have some sense of your goals, what motivates you and what makes your life worth living. The techniques are valuable once you have established a basis for choice.

★ **TRY THIS NOW!**
- *Identify your time robbers.*
- *Brainstorm what you might do about them.*
- *Select a solution and consider the implications for you and others.*
- *Implement your solution, then monitor and review its effect.*
- *Be prepared to make regular reviews of this nature.*

Identify which are:
- Urgent.
- Important.

Usually the proactive tasks help achieve results in your key areas. This is much less true of the reactive choices.

Next, schedule those activities:
- Proactive and important, giving time and emphasis according to their importance.
- Plan free time slots to fit in reactive activities. If they are urgent but not important get them out of the way quickly. If they are urgent and important you may have to reschedule.

The time robbers
When prioritizing activities the key questions to keep asking yourself are: 'What am I doing this for?', 'Is this the best way to use my time?', 'Do I really want to do this?' Watch out for:
- Personal disorganization. Use a diary, a filing system and plan to get help at organizing if you are poor at it.
- Overcommitment. Learn to prioritize, delegate and say 'no'. You may have to risk not being liked for a while.
- Intrusions. Take the telephone off the hook, close your door, have an appointment-only system, or tell people you are busy and when to come back.
- Meetings. Come prepared and demand the same of others, suggest more effective procedures, learn how to end meetings formally and politely.
- Custom and practice. Do not feel obliged to do things just because they have always been done. Review the routines and how often they need to be carried out, to clarify your expectations.
- Travel and waiting. Use this time to read, dream or write. Do not spend it fuming over the delay.
- Poor contracting. Be specific about when, where and how you expect work to be performed to avoid delay. Outline the consequences at the outset of a failure to meet the deadline.

While the suggestions mostly apply to work they may be adapted for home life. Remember, finding a satisfactory balance means negotiating with those who are likely to be affected.

WHEN THE BALANCE IS UNACCEPTABLE

It is important that you achieve a balance between work time, time you have to spend on maintaining yourself, and the discretionary or uncommitted time you have at your disposal. Equally, the time you spend in physical, mental and spiritual activity needs to be balanced for effective self-management.

There are occasions, however, when you rightly choose to place greater emphasis in time or energy expenditure on certain goals which could not otherwise be achieved. Most often this imbalance occurs in times of transition. A new home, new job, new relationship or child all demand more of your time and energy.

It is best to prepare other people for these situations, if possible. Prolonged imbalance of this kind is likely to damage your health, relationships and career prospects, not to mention your satisfaction in life.

To avoid the pitfalls, find ways of coping with the extra stress and tension which the imbalance will almost definitely cause.

When you are looking at ways of managing time and maintaining a balance in your life, you may notice that intentional imbalance occurs when you strive for particular goals. Further causes of imbalance, which normally occur unintentionally, are the crises and opportunities that take place as you grow up, mature and age.

WHAT ARE LIFE STAGES?

American writer Gail Sheehy describes such life stages in her book *Passages*. Getting to know what kinds of challenges you may face as you progress through those relatively predictable stages in your life can help you understand what is happening to you. It can enable you to be more prepared, and therefore more likely to benefit from the

Pulling up roots: 18–22

This period is usually characterized by movement out from the security of home toward becoming self-supporting. It requires some clarification of personal values to guide independent living. Often there is an attitude of 'I am not like my parents'.

The trying twenties

At this time there is usually a movement away from the inner turmoil of the struggle for personal identity and values and toward how to realize that identity in the other social world.

In finding this identity there is often a clash between going for safety and security and wanting to experiment.

There is often a fear that choices are irrevocable and set the scene for life. Rules tend to dominate thinking and action, and achieving intimacy and supportive relationships are important.

Catch 30

People often hit rock bottom around 30 and have a crisis or a re-evaluation of their life choices so far. Most seem to have outgrown the 'should motivated' choices of their twenties and reconnect with an inner dimension which they had avoided or ignored.

There is often a 180 degree turn, and a change of job, relationship and life direction.

Re-rooting: 30–35

The early thirties are typified by settling down, making it in your career, buying houses and having children. Long term goals tend to get set. There is a movement in relationships from the caring intimacy of the twenties to a greater centring on self-concern with a corresponding fall in mutuality.

This may be interpreted by your partner as indication that he or she is no longer loved, which may not be so. This is often further complicated by a reduced social life through having to care for children.

Deadline decade: 35–45

This life passage might usefully be understood in two linked phases. There is initially a sense of encroaching old age, which tends to sharpen ambitions. This is often experienced as the last chance to pull away from the pack or to become a parent.

There is a strong desire to establish one's individuality apart from the group or society, or to be outstanding in one's field. There is a tension between aspirations and achievement and a corresponding

challenge of boundaries, taking the initiative and a lessened anxiety to please.

Later this can be replaced with a sense of disillusionment and disappointment. Questions which are asked include 'What am I doing this for?' and 'Is this all there is?'

This re-evaluation (often called the midlife crisis) can be painful and disorienting. There is a grieving for the old self which is being let go and a vulnerable integration of those rejected parts of yourself to form a new unique identity.

seemingly inevitable rights of passage.

The following is a summary of Sheehy's life stages. The chronology is only approximate, and may vary slightly from person to person.

At 18 years of age, you will have already been through childhood separation from your mother, and experienced movement away from family toward peers and the establishment of sexual identity. It is important to realize that these 'growth issues' or opportunities may or may not be grasped by the individual.

If they are not grasped they often pop up later in life, when they cause problems or demand resolution. The same is true for those life tasks relate to the stages which follow.

The comeback decade

For those who fail to grasp or avoid the nettle of the midlife transition there is often staleness and rigidity, plus abandonment and despair. There is a letting up of the struggle to succeed and, for those who have undergone transformation, a greater acceptance of what one has. New coping strategies and new interests are developed and a greater balance achieved between work and leisure.

The freestyle fifties

This period usually results in greater autonomy once the children have grown up. There is greater opportunity for being together in relationships and solitude is more valued. There is often a questioning of values around God, mortality, money and time toward the end of the fifties.

Selective sixties

In your sixties you exercise more selectivity with regard to life, loves and friends. Energy is, for the most part, expended on what matters and on allowing yourself to be who you are.

Those who have been wise will have cultivated wider interests since the midlife transition and will find the switch from work to retirement a satisfying one to look forward to.

Thoughtful seventies

Often, there is a renewed interest in the mysteries of the world. This may be reflected in new courses of study or the passing on of your accumulated wisdom to the new generation.

Proud to be eighties

This period is often characterized by the ageing process. Those who use their faculties have a rich inner life. They feel there is still much to live for and a pride in surviving. There is a tension between autonomy, giving aid and surrendering to the need to receive the comfort and support necessitated by the ageing process.

There is a greater coming to terms with death, including a readiness and acceptance of its inevitability, though it may still be many years off.

MANAGING LIFE'S STAGES

Knowing yourself, being aware of what is happening to you, and staying in touch with it, no matter how painful, will help you manage these stages better.

By knowing a little of life's predictable stages you will at least realize when you have entered each new phase. It will help you to understand that it will pass with delightful consequences if you meet its challenge. Do not be afraid to get help. Counselling and psychotherapy are for normal people who want to change and transform themselves.

It is important to look after yourself. You are the only one you can absolutely trust. Moving from one stage to the next means consciously leaving the past behind. Looking for the benefits of your new stage will help you deal with the loss of the old.

People often associate learning with school, being young, inexperienced and vulnerable. Many, especially those who had a rough ride through the education system, associate it with boring or meaningless academic activity which did very little for their self-esteem and failed to give them credit for abilities which they may have been lucky enough to discover later.

The more successful may have come away with notions that learning and acquiring knowledge are about studying what is in books, that only the intelligent can learn, and that you finish learning before starting your career and adult life. These experiences and beliefs tend to deter people from getting involved in further learning and development.

WHY CONTINUE LEARNING?

The early education you received, whether good or bad, is simply not enough to help you cope with the complexity of modern life. Uncertainty in employment, redundancy, career moves, the rate of technical change and more leisure time all contribute to the shortfall. It is now clear that education is a lifelong affair and that it is not only work related.

Adults engage in education and training for many reasons. It may be for:

● Professional development, to gain recognition, security, job satisfaction, promotion or success.
● Personal development, to be able to relate better, to be better parents, more creative, healthier, happier, more influential or to get in charge of your life.
● Interest and adventure, to satisfy curiosity, excitement and novelty, seek peak experiences and a heightened sense of awareness.
● Dissatisfaction, if you feel you have outgrown your job, relationship, community, way of living, or feel jealous and envious.

THE ROLE OF THE LEARNER

As a child you had to adjust to society. You were relatively powerless and had little say over what you learned, how you learned it and how your learning was assessed. Many adults believe that this is how it will be if they return to some form of learning, but for a variety of reasons it is not.

Adults are not as dependent financially, emotionally or legally as children, and they are less willing to put up with inappropriately autocratic, didactic education. Adult learners demand that the richness and variety of their past experience be honoured and utilized.

They are demanding more say in what they are going to learn and how they will learn it. They are becoming active seekers instead of passive recipients and are more collaborative rather than competitive with their peers. They are also more likely to be internally motivated rather than relying on external reward or sanctions.

Teachers are becoming facilitators of learning rather than knowledge banks. They take more notice of learners' needs and act as resources and guides. Their teaching is more likely to be task and problem centred.

PATHWAYS

There are many pathways to learning. For example, you can use any one or combination of the following:

● Individualized learning.
● On the job training.
● Joining a course.
● Learning from life.

People have different learning styles, which often relate to their personality type or tendency. For example, feeling types like learning by immersion in doing; sensation types by means of active experimentation; intuitive types by reflective observation; thinking types lean toward abstract conceptualization.

Ideally, you should be competent in all modes, but this takes time and practice. Build on your strengths and identify your preferred learning style. Start using that mode and build the others as you learn. Your choice of any of the above pathways may depend on your preferred learning style.

STEPS IN LEARNING

If you join a course much of the following may already be structured for you, but if you are designing and managing your own learning the following points are worth noting.

It may surprise you to know that most adults learn on their own using the following methods, even if they are not very systematic about it.

What do you want to learn?

You may already have some ideas about the kind of changes you wish to make. If you do not, try using self tests, job interviews, appraisal, feedback or career counselling.

Define specific objectives

For each topic or area define the general objectives and the specific outcomes you desire. It is useful to decide whether you want a change in knowledge, attitudes and beliefs, and/or skills.

Decide steps and sequence

Break down learning into manageable units. Decide the order, if any, in which learning needs to take place.

How will you do it?

What learning activities and resources will you need? These might include workshops, books, self help groups and video tapes. Check your local educational institutions for courses and advice.

What help do you need?

You might find you need a tutor or a mentor. If so, you might be able to use local librarians, your boss, a colleague or the personnel and training officers of your company.

What constraints are operating?

There may be a number of constraints, including family commitments, limited time or resources, poor communication skills or poor concentration. You may have to do something about these or you may be able to find ways around them. Otherwise, in the last resort only, you may have to temper your expectation of what you can achieve.

How are you doing?

Occasionally you need to assess your learning to make sure you are progressing, to check standards and to identify where to put your energy next.

Most people who work learn on the job. Learning opportunities arise through new jobs, new projects, promotions and in-house training. Most of this learning is experiential and can be greatly improved by actively seeking out such opportunities and systematically using an experimental learning cycle such as that below.

Implied here is that you not only learn but learn how to learn. This makes for more efficient and effective learning – what is often called intelligence.

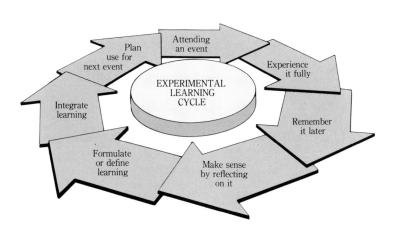

For most people, problem solving means applying learned solutions to familiar problems. However, this is obviously not enough when you do not know the answer, when the problem is unfamiliar, or when there is no right way of solving the problem and there are a number of possible solutions. In these cases you will need a strategy or a systematic problem solving process to tackle the dilemma effectively.

One such method, mentioned in Mapping Your Life (see pp. 12–27), is force field analysis. Briefly, this method consists of identifying all the forces acting in favour of the direction you wish to take and all those acting against your chosen direction.

You then look at ways of inhibiting the forces against, and increasing the forces for, the desired courses of action, usually paying attention to the major forces to start with.

THE PROBLEM SOLVING CYCLE

The problem solving cycle is another method you can use.

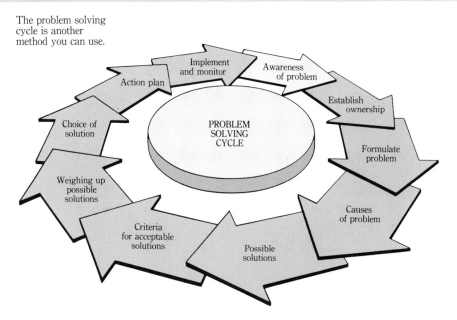

Awareness of the problem
You first need to list all the relevant details of the problem that you are aware of. This will include how you identify it as a problem, including the symptoms and effects.

Establish ownership
Once you have raised awareness of the nature and details of the problem, you need to find out whose problem it is. If it is not your problem it is not your business to solve it.

However, if it is not yours, you may have a separate problem arising from the fact that it is not being sorted out by someone else. Solve your own problems, not those of others. If it is a shared problem you need to work at it together.

★ REMEMBER!

In working through the cycle you may find that your perspective on the problem changes as you deepen your understanding. It may mean, for instance, *that the cause or a new solution appears in later stages or that the problem you thought you had is not really the problem at all, and you formulate a new one.* *Consulting others, sharing how far you have got, or seeking advice may be important if you feel the need. It may not be necessary to go through the whole* *process for each problem, but it is useful to know how if you need to. It may seem tedious at first but will become easier and speedier with practice.*

Formulating a problem
The best way of formulating a problem is in the form of a question aimed at your anticipated goal. For example, 'How can I get this job done?' rather than 'I can't get him to do what he agreed'.

It is important to formulate the problem to ensure that a successful conclusion is within your control rather than in someone else's hands.

Causes
Identify the possible causes of the problem. Brainstorm if necessary, then limit your list to the most probable or potent causes. The causes may often indicate the best avenues to a solution, and the chosen solution will need to be checked to see if it addresses the causes.

Possible solutions
Brainstorm a list of possible solutions. Do not evaluate or judge at this stage. No regard for feasibility should limit your suggestions.

Criteria for acceptable solutions
By setting out the hallmarks or requirements of a good solution at this stage you will know when you have succeeded in finding one. It will also help you to be clear about the basis on which you are making your final choice. These criteria will usually relate to the symptoms, effects and causes outlined above.

Weighing up possible solutions
This stage entails examining the pathway, the outcome and the implications or consequences of the various solutions. You will look at the feasibility and the timing of each solution, and generally deliberate on their advantages and disadvantages.

It is important not to dismiss options that may seem unrealistic. They may have elements of value which might be incorporated in the final choice.

Choice of solution
Choosing a solution means relinquishing other possibilities. More than one solution may be needed in sequence or simultaneously. When choosing your solution it is best to consider it from various angles, for example, thinking, feeling, sensation and intuition.

Does the solution fit in with your analysis of the problem? Does it fit with your gut reaction/your values? Does it address the facts in your awareness? Is it practical? How does it compare with your 'hunch' about what the right solution is?

Action plan
Your action plan will need to define the goal, that is the solution, and break it down into the stages or subtasks necessary to effect it. The plan will need to set target dates and indicate precisely how you intend to achieve your goal.

It will also need to specify the materials and human resources required., Finally, it will need to indicate standards against which you will identify your level of success. (See also Getting Things Done pp. 112–123.)

Implementing and monitoring
You now put your solution into action and monitor it according to the success criteria you have defined. You may need to adapt or compromise your solution in the light of information gained from monitoring.

Sometimes the action planning is only useful if the situation is stable and predictable.

If the situation is uncertain or unstable, then going into action may give rise to more information, which in turn results in a modification of the action. This process may be continued in an 'action, review, plan, action, review, plan' sequence until the solution is attained.

Everyone suffers from stress at some time, but learning certain skills to manage stress will enable you to function more effectively. You will be able to cope with the current stresses in your life, develop your ability to use your energy more efficiently, take on responsibilities you never thought you would be able to cope with, and discover talents you never dreamed you possessed.

In addition, learning to manage stress will make your relationships at work and at home more exciting and mutually supportive. You will be able to make changes in your life that lead to more stimulation, fulfilment and contentment. Increasing your awareness of the effects of stress in both your personal and work environments can help you to counter its more detrimental outcomes. You can then develop and broaden your range of skills to deal with stress more imaginatively and successfully.

WHAT IS STRESS?

Stress can be defined as the experience of unpleasant over- or under-stimulation, which actually or potentially leads to ill health.

No human being can function without stimulation and challenge. It is part of life and provides excitement, impetus and motivation, as well as distress and anxiety.

As long as you feel in control, challenge can be invigorating. However, with some of the challenges you meet, the more disabling feelings and actions associated with stress can take hold.

Stress is the result of a mismatch between the challenges you experience and your belief in your ability to cope. The challenges may come from sources external to you and may be the result of too much or too little pressure. They may also come from within you, and be a product of your own value systems, needs and expectations.

Everyone has powerful personal histories which affect their attitudes and actions. Therefore, everyone perceives and interprets stress in different ways.

★ TEST YOURSELF!

Stress can affect you in four different ways. This could be:
- *Physically, causing headaches or stomach upsets.*
- *Emotionally, creating tension and irritability.*
- *Mentally, by impairing logical thinking.*
- *Behaviourally, by affecting the way you act.*

Write down the ways in which you have been affected by stress. In which of the four categories are you affected most? Are you taking enough notice of the other signs?

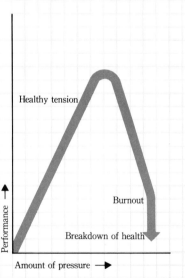

THE HUMAN FUNCTION CURVE

Healthy tension

Burnout

Breakdown of health

Performance →

Amount of pressure →

★ REMEMBER!

It is important to develop certain skills to deal with stress and keep on the upward slope of the human function curve. The way you deal with stress is an individual process. No one method will work for everyone.
- *Notice early signs of stress before they become too acute.*
- *Achieve the right balance between the amount of challenge in your life and your resources for dealing with it.*
- *Balance and expand the range of methods you use for dealing with stress.*

THE EFFECTS OF STRESS

However well you appear to cope with everyday life, you will experience stress to some degree. Moderate amounts are good for you, and can improve your performance, your efficiency and productivity. But too much may generate disabling emotions such as overwhelming anxiety and tension, difficulty in thinking clearly, and a wide range of behavioural responses.

The human function curve (*below left*) highlights the concept of healthy tension. The upward curve operates when you feel good, perform well, and can easily cure tiredness by periods of rest. The downward curve represents the slope toward burnout.

Burnout is a progressive condition, characterized by a loss of idealism, energy and purpose. It has been described as a syndrome of physical and emotional exhaustion, involving the development of negative job attitudes and a loss of concern and feeling for those with whom you work or are close to. The burnout scale provides a framework within which to assess the severity or extent of stress, both in yourself and in colleagues.

The fourth stage of burnout is dangerous. You have no reserves left to cope with any added pressure, and the slightest additional stress can send you hurtling into severe mental or physical breakdown. Yet the transition to that stage may be gradual and difficult to ascertain.

★ WHERE ARE YOU ON THE BURNOUT SCALE?

Stage 1
Lots of energy and enthusiasm.
Overconscientious, overworked.
Feelings of uncertainty.
Doubts about coping.

Warning signs
● Too busy to take holidays.
● Reluctant to take days off.
● Bringing work home.
● Too little time with partner/family.
● Frustrated with results.
● Unable to refuse more work.

Stage 2
Short-lived bouts of irritation.
Tiredness and anxiety.
Feelings of stagnation.
Blaming others.

Warning signs
● Complaints about the quality of other people's work.
● Unable to cope with pressure of work commitments.
● Working long hours.
● Unable to manage time efficiently.
● Too many social or work commitments.

Stage 3
General discontent.
Increasing anger/resentment.
Lowering of self-esteem.
Growing guilt.
Lack of emotional commitment.
Apathy.

Warning signs
● Lack of enjoyment of life.
● Extreme exhaustion.
● Reduced commitment to work.
● Reduced commitment at home.

Stage 4
Withdrawal.
Illness.
Feelings of failure.
Extreme personal distress.

Danger signs
● Increasing absenteeism.
● Avoiding colleagues.
● Reluctance to communicate.
● Increasing isolation.
● Physical ailments.
● Alcohol or drug abuse.

Stress is never the result of one single cause. Instead, it is created by a number of interrelated factors such as pressure at work, too many social commitments, an uncomfortable living or working environment, or an inability to organize and manage your time effectively.

In order to decide on the most appropriate strategies for dealing with the stress in your life, you first need to establish the main contributing factors.

THE STRESS CASCADE

Using the diagram below, ask yourself to what extent your stress is caused by the following factors:
● Individual: caused by your own beliefs, emotions, ways of thinking and acting.
● Interpersonal: related to specific people with whom you have contact.
● Organizational: specific to the particular organization in which you work.
● Community: specific to the locality in which you live or work.
● Cultural: arising from commonly accepted values, ways of living or expectations of people in particular roles.
● National: applicable to the country in which you live.
● International: in which world issues affect you.
● Universal: stresses that apply to every single human being.

Analysing the causes of stress in this way can sometimes leave you feeling helpless, since the problems you face can appear so unsurmountable. However, it is possible to reduce the stress in your life.

First, learn to make realistic action plans. Act on the stressors over which you can have the most influence. If it is your home or workplace that is affecting you, make the necessary changes and improvements. You do not need to do everything at once; take it in small steps.

Even with the most extensive stressor, you can do *something*. If national or international events or situations cause you to become stressed, you can raise money or contribute to a charitable organization which attempts to deal with the problem. This takes very little time and effort on your part, but can help to reduce your feeling of helplessness, and thus your stress.

You do not have to do it alone. Just talking to a friend, writing a memo, or a letter to someone in power is one small step that also reduces helplessness. This will help to lighten your load and reduce the stress that is associated with coping alone.

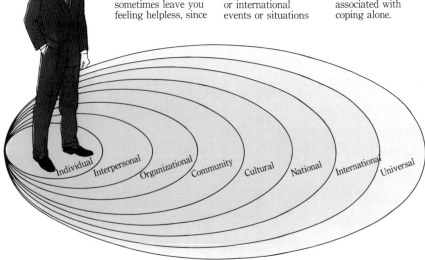

Individual Interpersonal Organizational Community Cultural National International Universal

CAUSES OF STRESS

Individual

- Unrealistic expectations of self.
- Inability to manage time efficiently.

- Lack of organization.
- Feelings of inadequacy.
- Under- or over-estimating abilities.

- Need to be in control.
- Inability to delegate.

- Inability to set limits, for example by saying no.
- Financial concerns.

Interpersonal

- Being required to fulfil others' expectations.
- Demands for perfection from family, superiors.

- Lack of autonomy at work.
- Dealing with aggressive or manipulative people.

- Lack of respect from others.
- Being taken for granted.
- Not being involved in decision-making.

Organizational

- Poor professional communication systems.
- Extremes of management style.
- Working with an inexperienced staff.

- Lack of clarity and agreement about the values and goals of the organization.
- Lack of consideration for the individual within the organization.

- Lack of positive and/or critical feedback to employees.
- Inadequate staffing levels for the job at hand.

- Lack of team and organizational identities.
- Highly competitive structures.

Community

- Inadequate local services.
- Noise pollution.
- Traffic congestion.
- Lack of space.
- Lack of a sense of community.
- High crime rates.

Cultural

- Racial, religious and sexual prejudice and discrimination.
- Rigid expectations of certain types of behaviour from people according to their gender, class or status irrespective of their individuality.

National

- Government policies affecting defence, the economy, unemployment, public services, taxation and rates.
- Civil unrest.
- National disasters.
- War and the threat of war.

International

- Difficulties in understanding different values, politics, cultures.
- Migration.
- War and disasters in other countries.
- Environmental damage affecting large parts of the entire planet.

Universal

- The experience of being vulnerable.
- Accepting the frailty of the human body.

- Having to sacrifice some individuality to function in a group, partnership or team.

- The transitions that must be made as you grow older.
- Spiritual ambiguities.

- The comparative insignificance of the individual human within the universe.
- The inevitability of death.

When learning to cope with stress, you must balance the methods that you use. First, you must assess the resources you already have that can be used to manage stress. Then, you need to plan how to build on them.

Avoid the exclusive use of any one particular method. An over-reliance on and overuse of any one means of coping can cause more problems than it solves. For example, sleeping pills or alcohol to help you relax can be valuable on an occasional basis, but daily use leads to sluggishness and addiction.

By the time you reach adulthood you will probably have developed your own individual stress toolkit, which is your set of coping strategies that work for you. You may find, however, that organizational and social change, as well as your individual process of getting older, can render your well-established coping mechanisms ineffective. And this may happen before you realize it.

BALANCE THE METHODS

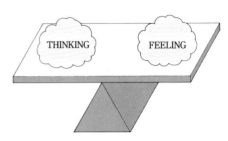

You need to have a wide variety of coping strategies in order to be able to manage each stressful situation appropriately. It is important that you aim to achieve a balance between the various means you use. In the same way that specific methods can be overused, over-reliance on certain types of methods can, in turn, lead you to further stress.

For example, a person who relies too much on tackling problems head on but does not allow himself to express his feelings can become exhausted and emotionally distant, even from the people to whom he is supposed to be closest. Someone who is unable to nuture himself, but is expert at distracting himself by helping other people with their problems, will find that he becomes drained and overwhelmed by endless demands.

The table opposite indicates four categories of methods of dealing with stress; these categories need to be balanced for you to effectively manage stress. Some of the methods listed can be used before, during or after a specific stressful event, and some are means of dealing with the stress of life in general. Others can perform both functions.

Use the categories to determine which types of stress control you are already practising, and which areas you are weak in and need to develop further.

You may find that you are terrific at active distraction but rarely ever practice self-nurturing. You may also find that you rely too heavily on one of the areas and ignore the others. The secret of managing stress is to balance all of the methods, using every type that is available.

★ TEST YOURSELF!

To assess your strengths and weaknesses you should determine how balanced your stress toolkit is. Managers are often strong in actively tackling the problem and active distraction categories but weak in others.
● *Make a list of the ways in which you have dealt with stress to date, including the many ordinary, everyday methods.*
● *Delete those which you consider negative, and which result in more stress in the future.*
● *Look at the examples in the table and add to your list any which apply to you.*
● *Categorize the methods on your list under the headings in the table.*
● *Notice which categories are your strongest and which are your weakest.*
● *Identify the methods of dealing with stress you most need to develop, or need to use more often in order to achieve a better balance in your stress toolkit.*

★ REMEMBER!

Once you have learned to balance the different categories of stress control, you will find that these new skills enable you to:

- *Raise your energy level.*
- *Develop your potential to take on more responsibility.*

- *Use talents you may not be aware of.*
- *Improve your relationships at work and at home.*

- *Initiate changes which help you to develop as a person.*

WAYS TO DEAL WITH STRESS

TACKLING A PROBLEM

Thinking
Analysing the problem; brainstorming solutions; deciding priorities and goals; planning; obtaining information or resources.

Utilizing other people
Asking for help or advice; asserting your wants and needs; challenging someone causing the stress.

The organization/ system
Telling people in power your views; helping them make a case for change; joining a political group.

ACTIVE DISTRACTION

People
Conversing about topics not related to source of stress; helping someone else.

Hobbies
Activities that keep you mentally and physically busy; physical exercise.

SELF-NURTURING

Rest
Taking proper breaks; relaxation exercises; getting away from stressful situations; holidays or weekends away.

Diet
Eating proper meals; eating foods that please you; restricting intake of alcohol, caffeine and other drugs.

Luxuriating
Buying something special; meeting friends for a drink or a meal; a hot bath; taking a sauna; having a massage.

EMOTIONAL EXPRESSION

Expressing your feelings verbally
Unburdening to a friend, colleague or counsellor; writing down your uncensored feelings, then tearing up the paper; joining a support group.

Catharsis
Having a good cry; letting off steam without abusing anyone; screaming, swearing or shouting into a pillow or in the privacy of a car.

Creative emotional expression
Writing poetry; painting; writing; sculpting; playing a musical instrument; singing; dancing.

If you take the time to learn some simple relaxation exercises you will find that you will be able to combat the fatigue and lack of concentration that accompany stress. The physical tension that comes with stress is a waste of effort and energy. It dulls your mind and makes you tire more quickly.

Tension reduces the blood supply to your muscles, causing a build-up of waste products and a variety of aches and pains. The circulatory system has to work harder to get the blood around your body and can result in high blood pressure.

You may find that if you are constantly under stress and tension you begin to accept the reactions they evoke, and may find it difficult to notice their presence or effects. Your sense of what feels relaxed becomes distorted.

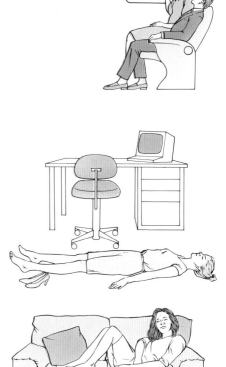

LEARN TO PAUSE

The art of relaxation not only includes relaxing at the end of the day, at the weekend or on holiday, but also involves being able to pause frequently throughout the day.

Busy people can get into the habit of over-reacting to stimuli. Or it may be that you find yourself on the go all the time, unable to slow down when there is a lull or a break. This is the road to burnout.

If you practise pausing you can prevent yourself being caught in this trap. Pausing can clear your mind, reduce some of your habitual tensions and help you make more efficient use of your time and energy. Pauses can be taken anywhere, and need last a few minutes at the very most.

Use the 10-second pause at the beginning and the end of each task or section of a task.

The five-minute pause gives your mind and body a chance to rest and recharge. Use it while travelling, when someone keeps you waiting, during coffee breaks, or at home after work.

Try to fit at least three five-minute pauses into the most active part of your day. You will find it easier to summon the energy for the next phase of work and your life outside work, and easier to get to sleep at night. The last of these might seem surprising, but short relaxation pauses during the day prevents the overstimulation of your system that can lead to insomnia.

THE 10-SECOND PAUSE

This can be done anytime, and anywhere. Make a conscious effort to have plenty of these pauses throughout the day.

● Breathe in slowly and deeply to the count of five, expanding your abdomen as you do so.

● Put both feet flat on the floor and your hands in your lap.

● Breathe out slowly to the count of five, maintaining the spinal stretch that happened as you breathed in.

● Let your breathing become natural and get on with the next task at hand.

THE FIVE-MINUTE PAUSE

Before you begin, try to ensure that you will not be interrupted for five minutes. Sit with your feet flat on the floor and your knees comfortably apart. Place your hands in your lap. Keep the base of your spine at the back of the chair, with your back upright and your head balanced. Close your eyes.

● Take a slow deep breath in, expanding your abdomen, then slowly breathe out.

● Focus in turn on each part of your body, paying particular attention to your head and hands. Imagine that each part is becoming warm and relaxed. Keep your spine upright.

● Start with the back of your head, working behind the ears. Then relax the top of your head, forehead, eyelids,

eyes, and face. Keep your jaw slightly open and your tongue from touching the top of your mouth.

● Work down your throat, neck and shoulders. Concentrate on your arms, starting with the right. Work around the hand, from the palm through each of your fingers and up the arm to your shoulder. Feel each part of your arm relaxing as you do so.

● Relax your shoulders, then work down your left arm and hand in the same order as you did your right.

● Now relax your back, abdomen, pelvis, buttocks, legs and feet.

● Take one more slow deep breath in and out.

● Stretch your hands and feet and open your eyes.

DEEP RELAXATION

This takes considerably longer than pausing, but should be performed at least once a day when you are under stress. It takes about 20 to 30 minutes and you need to be sitting or lying down with the whole of your body supported, preferably on a flat, hard surface.

With practice, you can learn deep relaxation of your body and your mind. This will significantly enhance your mental and physical energy. It will also result in more restful sleep at night and even save time by reducing the amount of sleep you need.

There are a variety of methods for deep relaxation. They help you to focus your attention on various parts of the body, and to instruct the muscles in that area to relax at a deeper and deeper level. Individuals develop different preferences;

one method may help you to relax more than others.

Initially using relaxation tapes can be a useful way of learning the skill. Eventually you will be able to do it without the tape. Ensure that any commercially-produced tape has a voice and background music that you find soothing. Alternatively, you can make your own relaxation tape.

To do this, expand and write down the five-minute pause exercise as if it were a script. Tell yourself what to do step-by-step. Have the entire sequence repeated three times. Ask someone whose voice you find relaxing to tape record your script, reading it more and more slowly as he progresses. Arrange for your favourite relaxing music to be recorded in the background.

★ REMEMBER!

Practise your relaxation techniques, and gradually build up the time you spend using them. Like most other methods of dealing with stress, relaxation needs to be practised to achieve a level of skill.

At first, use the techniques during periods when you are

not feeling particularly stressed. People who are very stressed often complain that they have no time to practise relaxation. However, relaxation exercises can save you time; you will be more energetic and efficient as a result.

All forms of stress have an emotional element, but the emotional energy created by stress can be used to your advantage. Emotions are resources which, when used with understanding and skill, will have a positive effect.

First of all, it is important to distinguish between thought, intuition, sensations and emotions. You will find that the word 'feeling' is often used to apply to these four distinct aspects of human functioning.

When your intention is to communicate emotions but you end up talking about thought, intuition or sensation, you will probably cross messages with the person you are addressing.

WHAT ARE EMOTIONAL SKILLS?

Emotional skills can be learned and developed. There is a common misconception that once a person reaches a state of 'maturity' they have learned all they can about emotions. However, just as you can develop new technical or intellectual skills, you can go on building your emotional skills. These skills include:

Control
Emotional control is an essential skill. There are many occasions when you need to hold back rather than hurt someone, or control your emotions during times of stress.

Awareness
This includes being aware of your own emotions and the extent to which they can influence behaviour. Awareness is essential so that you can selectively control emotions rather than put a blanket repression on all of them or express them too freely. This leaves room for choice about expressing emotions and using them as a resource.

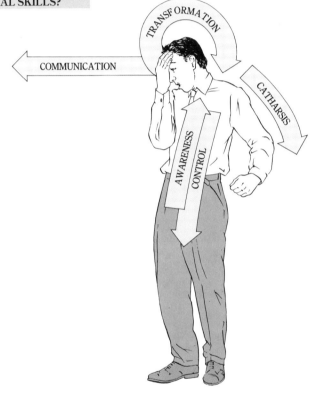

Communication
Self-disclosure helps to build trust in relationships. It includes taking the risk of sharing positive feelings, revealing your emotional vulnerability, and giving constructive criticism.

Catharsis
As a skill, this is a controlled process of letting go. You are aware of what you are doing and choosing to do it safely at the appropriate time and place. It is also called emotional release or letting off steam.

Transformation
This is the transformation of the energy of emotions into constructive thought or action. It is often called 'transmutation', a name that comes from the days of alchemy – the attempt to turn base metal into gold.

HOW TO BUILD EMOTIONAL SKILLS

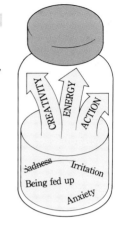

To improve and build on these important skills, there are a number of steps you can take. Some you may already be competent at, while others may need some practice.

Control
● Learn breathing, relaxing and meditation techniques so that when you are under stress you can easily use them to control your emotions and responses.
● Remove yourself from the stressful situation to collect yourself.
● Change the subject to something you are more comfortable with to give you time to regain control of yourself.
● Focus on the positive aspects of what is going on, even if they are minor.

Awareness
● Accept that you are allowed to have emotions.
● Notice the areas of tension in your body. They will often help you realize how you are really feeling.
● Realize that you can feel more than one emotion at one time, and that these emotions may be contradictory.
● Notice how particular emotions affect your actions.

Communication
● Practise finding words that describe what and how you are feeling.
● Start lightly peppering your ordinary conversation with words which describe pleasant feelings and mildly difficult ones.
● Share some of your warm emotions with other people.
● When you feel vulnerable, ask someone just to listen while you get a problem off your chest. Explain that you do not expect them to find a solution or say anything in particular.
● When you feel uncomfortable with someone, tell them how you feel.

● Take an interest in how other people feel, but do not probe farther than the level corresponding to your own willingness to make parallel revelations about yourself. Do not give advice unless you are asked for it. Listen, and do not criticize, when someone is talking about their feelings.

Catharsis
● Pick an appropriate time and place to let off steam cathartically.
● If you are not used to catharsis, carry out very short periods at first, using control techniques to get yourself out of it each time.
● Go through the motion of some of the cathartic techniques even if they do not feel spontaneous. Being in control of letting go is a skill which needs practice.
● Scream and shout into a pillow, or out loud if you will not be overheard, when you are feeling most pent up.
● Save up cracked crockery in an easily accessible place. Get it out and smash it noisily when you feel pent up.
● Bash or kick cushions, your mattress, or cardboard boxes.

Transformation
● Move around physically to unblock your energy, then proceed to do something constructive. For

example, if worrying about a report, go for a brisk walk, then start it immediately.
● Pour out your feelings into something creative.
● Gradually up your body fitness. You can then use vigorous exercise to do something useful when under stress.
● Learn deep meditation skills in which you can change the feelings into creative ideas.

★ REMEMBER

Learning how to harness your emotional energy will give you the ability to be more dynamic in your work and your personal life.

Building emotional skills will give you more energy, stamina and creativity. It will also help you establish more interesting and supportive relationships.

MANAGING YOURSELF AND OTHERS

THE IMPORTANCE OF COMMUNICATION

Communication is a key to success in your work and in your social interactions. You need communication skills and strategies to share ideas and experiences, to find out about things that interest you, and to explain to people what you want.

Developing ways of communicating, including language and nonverbal body signals, is essential if you are to express your feelings and insights. Learning to communicate effectively may mean the difference between barely coping with life as you know it and actively shaping your world as you would like it to be.

WHAT IS GOOD COMMUNICATION?

You can get some idea about what good communication is by studying what good communicators do. They:

● Know what they want to say.
● Can gain the attention of the recipient/listener.
● Can establish and maintain relationships.
● Know what the listener likes and is interested in.
● Choose how to communicate from a range of options.
● Are skilful in communicating.
● Choose when and where to communicate.
● Are clear, brief and coherent.
● Are active listeners.
● Can understand and clarify messages they receive.
● Do not get distracted.
● Know how to close a conversation or communication.

On the other hand, poor communicators are often not clear about what they want to say or to whom they wish to say it. They are not sufficiently aware of other people's needs or interests, and therefore communicate in inopportune times and places.

They are often not aware of their listeners while speaking, and fail to respond to the verbal and nonverbal feedback which tells them how the interaction is going.

The report looks good, doesn't it?

I feel terrible.

WHY DEVELOP COMMUNICATION SKILLS?

Good communication can enable you to make yourself known to others, to build friendships and create other types of satisfying relationships. Poor communication will often result in isolation, confusion, frustration, being ignored or resented.

Being a good communicator is about sending and receiving messages in the context of an open supportive relationship. You can send and receive messages by a variety of methods. However most people have difficulty with face to face communication.

It may seem strange, but people often forget that communication is about moving information from one person to another. They do not remember that the sender and receiver are different people with different needs, interests, goals and ways of seeing the world, which they must allow for when communicating.

THE IMPORTANCE OF RELATIONSHIPS

KEYS TO
RELATIONSHIPS

Empathy

Congruence

Unconditional
positive regard

Acceptance

Good communication requires open, supportive relationships. The relationship can be judged by the 'atmosphere' in which a communication takes place. If the atmosphere is stormy or full of static communication will be poor; if it is clear communication has a greater chance of being successful.

Open supportive relationships require that people:
● Are willing to give and take feedback.
● Value each other and want to spend time with them.
● Show a respect for the needs and interests of others.

● Are willing to talk openly about themselves where appropriate.
● Believe that most people will respond favourably when approached.
● Acknowledge other's rights to choose for themselves.
● Realize that they will not be liked by everyone.

Keys to relationships
A number of fundamental components to developing open supportive relationships have been identified.

● Empathy, which is the ability to sense the world from another person's point of view and feel the way they feel.
● Unconditional positive regard, or the belief that whoever you are with is basically 'okay' as a person. Their behaviour may not always endear them to you, but as a person they are or can be 'okay'.
● Congruence, which means being seen in the relationship as a person who says what he means and means what he says. It means being honest and giving a similar message at both verbal and nonverbal levels.

● Acceptance is the ability to acknowledge and relate to people as they really are, not as they should be or how you would like them to be. It means accepting them with all their faults and failings.

It is against this background of relationships, in which participants possess many of these qualities, that the most satisfying communication will take place. Poor communication is as likely to result from poor relationships as from inadequate sending and receiving skills. It is also true, however, that poor relationships will result from poor communication skills.

As well as the quality of the relationship, there are other factors which influence the effectiveness of communication. These are your self-image, your clarity of expression, the ability to listen, managing feelings, a willingness to learn and self-disclosure.

SELF-IMAGE

A major factor that affects your ability to communicate is your self-esteem (see pp. 28–37). This determines how you value yourself and what you have to say. If you do not think what you have to say is worthwhile, it is unlikely that others will take notice.

A person with high self-esteem has feelings of self-worth, confidence and adequacy. He is secure in himself, which permits him to express positive and negative feelings, to handle criticism, to challenge and confront, and to manage conflict.

Low self-esteem causes inferiority feelings, a lack of confidence and feelings of inadequacy. A person with low self-esteem may feel that he is uninteresting to others. He may have difficulty in conversing with others, admitting that he is wrong, expressing his feelings, accepting constructive criticism from others, or voicing ideas that are different in case he is disliked.

CLARITY OF EXPRESSION

This involves knowing what you want to say and how you want to say it. The good communicator is sensitive to the psychological signals in the environment and is clear about what he wishes to communicate.

The poor communicator usually has difficulty with clarity. First, he may lack an awareness of how to transmit messages effectively. He fails to present his message in words and language that convey his intended meaning, or fails to communicate audibly and clearly.

In addition, he may be unclear about what he is really trying to communicate. Instead of having organized ideas or intentions, the messages are haphazard, erratic and unplanned.

Finally, poor communicators assume that the recipients of their messages will have understood because they, themselves, can. And the poor communicators leave the listeners to guess what they mean.

LISTENING

Listening is much more than hearing. Hearing is the reception of auditory information. Listening is an intellectual and emotional process that decodes physical, intellectual and emotional input in a search for meaning and understanding. Effective listening occurs when the listener correctly understands the sender's meaning.

Unfortunately, few people are good listeners. About 75 percent of oral communication is ignored, misunderstood or quickly forgotten.

Effective listening is not a passive process. To be an effective listener:
● Have a reason for listening.
● Demonstrate skill in giving attention.
● Use silences and infrequent questions.
● Encourage the other person to talk.
● Suspend judgement.
● Wait before responding.
● Be able to repeat what the speaker says.
● Be able to rephrase, in your own words, what was said.
● Be ready to respond.
● Be ready to look behind the words for deeper messages.

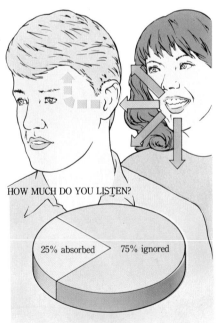

HOW MUCH DO YOU LISTEN?

25% absorbed   75% ignored

MANAGING FEELINGS

To be human is to experience a constant current of changing emotions and feelings. By and large however, in this particular phase of Western culture most people often have difficulties in handling the emotional side of their nature. This results in very real communication difficulties.

Because people learn to suppress their emotions two developments are likely to have occurred:
● You do not always know what your emotions are.
● You do not have the skills of expressing emotion.

However, expression of emotions is important in building good relationships with others. People need to express their feelings in such a manner that they influence, affirm, reshape, and change themselves – and others. In order to achieve this the following guidelines are helpful.
● Be aware of your emotions. Identify them correctly.
● Give yourself permission to experience your emotions.
● Accept your emotions. They are a valuable part of you.
● Share your emotions. Deep communication is not possible unless you do this.
● Balance your emotions with other aspects of yourself, such as your mind and will, when communicating.

SELF-DISCLOSURE

The ability to talk truthfully and fully about oneself is necessary to effective communication. Every individual is rich in sensitivities, experiences, emotions, thoughts and ideas.

In order to be known by others you must be willing and able to self-disclose when appropriate. This is a mutual process – the more two people know about each other the more effective and efficient the communication can be.

There are many blocks to self-disclosure. Most people have fears and doubts about their acceptability to others. They fear rejection or miscomprehension, or they fear that they are unworthy, which causes them to fear self-disclosure.

It is important to replace fear with trust. No one is likely to engage in much self-disclosure in a threatening situation, and the effective communicator is one who can create an environment of trust in which mutual self-disclosure can occur.

WILLINGNESS TO LEARN

As you communicate you receive two sorts of message — those from others and those from within yourself. Effective communicators use both these types of feedback to learn about others, about the impact of their communications and communication style, and to learn about themselves. In addition, effective communicators watch others in order to learn about skills, techniques and personalities.

In consequence, the total communication experience is always a potential learning experience also. Effective communicators learn from their mistakes and are ready to try out new ways of communicating. In contrast, the poor communicator is not actively engaged in learning. All the valuable data to enhance self-understanding, effective relating and good communication is missed.

TWO TYPES OF FEEDBACK

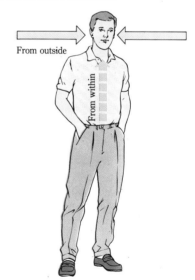

From outside

from within

★ REMEMBER!

Do not repress your emotions. They are best identified, observed, accepted and integrated. You can then discover more about who you are, and can share yourself with those around you.

Communication is basically an interaction or a transaction between two people who are separate individuals with different needs, goals, outlooks and values. Some interactions are productive, constructive and satisfying, while others are destructive and result in one or both parties being dissatisfied. Transactional analysis provides a tool for discriminating between good and bad transactions, and helps to predict which kinds will lead to satisfying outcomes.

All good transactions achieve a satisfactory completion of the task and maintain or enhance the relationship within which the transaction takes place. Both people end up a winner, feeling 'I'm okay, you're okay'.

ANALYSING INTERACTIONS

To analyse your transactions you work with the premise that everyone has internalized or made part of themselves certain ways of relating with people. These are based mostly on the way you were brought up as a child. Such roles, or patterns of relating, are determined by psychological life scripts or deeply entrenched beliefs about who you are and what you are doing here.

The script reflects parental messages to the child. It relates to the child's perception of reality, how it works and their place in it. It is also closely connected with your concept of yourself and self-esteem. Your personal life script usually results in one of four psychological positions or stances from which you approach the world and your relationships with others. These are:
● 'I'm okay, you're okay.'
● 'I'm okay, you're not okay.'
● 'I'm not okay, you're okay.'
● 'I'm not okay, you're not okay.'
Only the first of these positions is likely to promote effective and satisfying communication. It is likely to have resulted from nurture and tender loving care. Structural nurturance, such as everyday greetings, helps maintain relationships at a tolerable level. Intimate and spontaneous positive nurture – for example careful listening or giving specific unexpected compliments – make people feel alert, alive, significant and worthwhile.

Discounting, which is negative nurture (or none at all), may result in the person taking up the 'not okay' positions. You discount people when you ignore, tease, degrade, ridicule, laugh at or humiliate them. You can also do it by denying the significance of their problems, the possibility of a solution, or their ability to find one.

Most discounting comes through body language, such as the note of disgust in the voice or the disapproving look in the eye.

Everyone needs nurture. You, and your relationships, will thrive by maximizing positive nurture and minimizing discounts.

I'm okay, you're okay.

I'm okay, you're not okay.

I'm not okay, you're okay.

I'm not okay, you're not okay.

★ REMEMBER!

To enhance the effectiveness of your communication, and ensure a more satisfying relationship or outcome:
● *Provide nurturance and strokes rather than discount.*
● *Maintain complementary transactions.*

THE EFFECT OF THE EGO

To understand your ways of relating, it will help if you can imagine that you have three different internal ego states – the parent, the adult and the child.

The parent figure in you is protective and nurturing, critical, advising, and can make all sorts of rules and regulations. The adult figure is a problem solver. It collects and analyses data and works out what you need and want. The child figures can be angry, rebellious, conforming, frightened, spontaneous, carefree and fun-loving.

The main value in the parent, adult, child system (PAC), as far as communication is concerned, is that it can help you discriminate between the helpful complementary transactions and unhelpful ones (sometimes called games).

If you look at the following transactions it will quickly become obvious what those terms mean, for example, a boss and secretary in a child/ nurturing parent transaction.
'I'm worried about getting this work in by our deadline.'
'Don't worry, I'll see if I can free Jill to help you.'

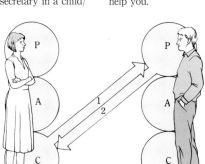

This is a helpful or parallel transaction because the secretary spoke from her 'child' position to her boss's nurturing 'parent'. He responded from his nurturing parent to her needy chid.

Similarly many other complementary transactions are possible, for example, parent to parent, child to child, adult to child.

I'm worried about getting this work done by our deadline.

Don't worry, I'll see if I can free Jill to help you.

In the following example we have a crossed transaction, when a boss comes to talk to his secretary.
'Let's go and see George's new computer.'
'Can't you ever keep an appointment?'
Here the child in the boss looked for a response from the child in his secretary but instead got a critical parent response. This is a crossed transaction and results in an unsatisfactory outcome for both. Crossed transactions can be:
● Indirect, for example one person talks to another in front of a third whom he hopes will 'get the message'.

● Diluted, where there is a double message given with affection and hostility.
● Weak, where there is little intensity of feeling.
Ulterior transactions are crossed transactions but are more complex, since the transaction takes place on two levels at once. One message is explicit and open, while the other is implied tacitly.

You can never be sure exactly what the message is when there are ambiguous or ulterior transactions.

Let's go and see George's new computer.

Can't you ever keep an appointment?

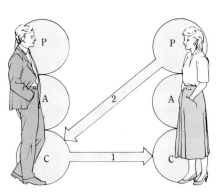

When communication has a particular intention, it may be helpful to consider a complete transaction, or face to face interaction, in terms of the stages or parts which highlight important features in the communication.

These eight stages may receive different emphasis in various transactions, but at one time or another each stage will be necessary for effective communication.

1 Preparing the message.
2 Preparing yourself.
3 Gaining attention or making contact.
4 Preparing the receiver.

5 Sending the message.
6 Receiving and clarifying the reply.
7 Closing communication.
8 Following it up.

PREPARING THE MESSAGE

It is surprising how many people communicate without knowing what it is they wish to achieve. Be aware of exactly what you want to communicate, and then check whether that is what you really want by asking yourself 'Why am I doing this?'

Having a clear-cut objective will help you keep on track and not lose your way through distraction. Be clear, brief and specific. Come to the point quickly, explanation can follow later.

The following checklist will help in preparing your message.
● What is the main message?
● Who is it for?
● What outcome do I want?
● How will I communicate?
● When is the best time?

● Where is the best place?
● Are the major points clear?
● Is there ambiguity?
● Are the facts correct?
● Is the action required clear?
● Does it include all the information they need to know?

PREPARING YOURSELF

If you do not value yourself it is unlikely that you will convey that your message is worth attending to.

Every time you speak you are presenting yourself. Nonverbal messages speak volumes about the kind of person you are and whether you value yourself or not. Try to convey this value by creating the environment which brings out the best in you and by being assertive.

GAINING ATTENTION

Having the expectation that somebody will respond positively when you attempt to gain their attention is essential.

Important communications are best not left to chance encounters, or times when there are other pressures or distractions.

In face to face communication you can attract attention by the following:

- Asking for it.
- Humour.
- Eye contact.
- Engaging listener's interest.
- Visual images.
- Vocal intensity.
- Body gestures and positioning.

- Personal appearance.

However you conduct your communication, make sure that you have the other person's attention before you begin your message.

PREPARING THE RECEIVER

If your message is shocking, or your listener is not expecting or ready for your message, you may need to spend time helping to prepare them. Useful ways include:
- Saying what you want to communicate.

- Saying what benefit they might gain as a result.
- Checking that they are willing to communicate.

- Warning them of the importance of your communications.
- Asking rhetorical questions to awaken curiosity.

SENDING THE MESSAGE

When you are in the process of relaying the message, keep in mind what you are communicating for. Use simple language, avoid unnecessary detail and emphasize the main points to aid the listener's understanding.

For impact, relate what you are saying to the emotions as well as the mind. While presenting your message:
- Speak audibly.
- Vary your pitch, tone and volume.
- Respond to signs of confusion or disinterest.
- Pause for questions

and clarification.
- Summarize to help understanding.
- Talk 'to' people, not 'at' them.
- Switch the approach if yours is not working.

RECEIVING AND CLARIFYING

Listening is the primary skill needed here (see pp 104–105). It is not simply 'not speaking', it is an active process of attending to the speaker.

Be aware of:
- Switching off from dull response or because you disagree.

- Getting hooked on detail or missing main points.
- Being preoccupied with your own problems and not

concentrating on what is said.
- Trying to win over the other person rather than give a fair hearing.

CLOSING A CONVERSATION

Often an interaction can become boring, stuck, destructive or simply have achieved its purpose. In such cases it is essential to have appropriate ways of finishing the transaction.

Some closure strategies include:
- A demand for

action or reaction.
- Suggesting ways forward.
- Summarizing what has been achieved.
- Arranging another

meeting.
- Indicating that you have finished.
- Thanking the person for their time.

FOLLOWING UP

In many cases effective communication needs to be followed up to get something done or to stay in touch and maintain the relationship.

In business, it is often useful to summarize face to face or telephone conversations in a memo for your own benefit, or for those who may be affected by it or need to be aware of information or decisions which have emerged.

When you communicate you need to have an overall aim. In addition, any communication requires various subgoals or objectives which you need to achieve as an interaction progresses.

You will need to use specific behaviours to communicate these intentions effectively to someone else. But first you must determine what it is you are trying to achieve when communicating.

WHAT ARE YOU TRYING TO ACHIEVE?

There are a number of goals that may apply to what you are trying to achieve when you communicate. Your communications can be:

- Prescriptive, which seek to give direction and help make someone more self-directing.
- Informative, which seek to increase a person's knowledge and encourage independent thinking.
- Confronting, to challenge restrictive attitudes or behaviour, and helps a person to be more self-confronting.
- Cathartic, which facilitates release of tension or pent-up emotion and constructive management of emotional blockage.
- Catalytic, to accelerate a person's self-discovery processes and build trust in their ability to take charge of their own life.
- Supportive, which affirms a person's

worth and value and encourages them to celebrate and take pleasure in themselves and others.

The first three categories assume that you are speaking from an authoritative or expert position while the others do not. All are necessary for good communication. But different emphasis will be given to each depending on the outcome desired and the roles or relationship of the people involved.

Each category consists of a variety of specific skills, each of which serves a slightly different purpose. The skill, manner, timing and the form of words used need to be closely monitored to ensure that the communication is not degenerate. That is, is not manipulative, compulsive or unsolicited and does not infringe on the rights of others.

SPECIFIC SKILL EXAMPLES

The following are some specific examples of skills needed within each category.

Prescriptive

You can prescribe goals, methods, behaviour or values to someone. Of course, they do not have to take your prescription on board. They are free to use or reject all your interventions, though sometimes there may be consequences. If your message is prescriptive you might:

- Command, advise, propose or suggest.
- Evaluate or correct a person's work.
- Assign homework or responsibilities.
- Recommend action or research.

Prescription can be carried out in an autocratic fashion, or you might consult the person first. It should not be used if the person is capable of directing themselves appropriately and should not undermine their freedom of choice.

Informative

Some of the dangers to watch out for include giving information that is not wanted, rambling statements or inadequate exploration. Guard against oppression and dogma in your manner and the content of what you say.

- Clarify what information you wish to pass on.
- Choose the best time and place to give it.
- Determine what kind of information it will be, for example, rationale, interpretation, analysis or feedback.
- Decide the level and amount of information needed.
- Decide the best format, for example face to face, written, by telephone or tape.

Confronting

You should decide if the confrontation is for your benefit or the recipient's. Are you pussyfooting and avoiding, sledgehammering, or telling the truth lovingly? Remember, even loving confrontation results in discomfort or shock and must be backed up with support for the person. Techniques include:

● Give awareness-raising feedback.
● Direct questioning aimed at uncovering a hidden agenda.
● Playing devil's advocate to challenge when little evidence is available.
● Sharing appropriate anger to give the impression of importance and to give weight to confrontation.

Cathartic

Try out this kind of release yourself. Your subsequent ease and confidence will empower and reassure others.

● Give reassurance and permission to vent emotions in a way that is not destructive.
● Encourage shouting, laughing, storming, shaking and crying.
● Provide cushions for venting anger and physical touch where necessary.
● Help a person verbalize their insights following emotional release.
● Help a person to take their attention away from their distress through switching the activity, such as counting backward or using humour.

Catalytic

This kind of communication is used to show another person how to do something, not to do it for them. Make maximum use of their enlisting abilities.

● Reflect back words or phrases to encourage them.
● Check for understanding and summarize occasionally.
● Ask open or closed questions to initiate or focus a response.
● Offer self-discovery structures, for example problem-solving and learning cycles.
● Help a person map out their present understanding.

Supportive

When being supportive do not be judgemental, take over or rescue someone.

● Give your undivided attention and listen actively.
● Encourage, praise, appreciate, affirm.
● Celebrate their ideas, appearance, values and behaviour.
● Be genuine and honest in expressing care and concern.
● Touch supportively in a nurturing way.
● Share your own strengths and weaknesses.
● Do something for the person, or offer assistance.

★ TEST YOURSELF!

Examine your own skills in each of the six categories and assess your strengths and weaknesses.
● *In which categories do you need to develop your skills?*
● *Do you use any of the categories in a manipulative, compulsive or unsolicited way?*
   You can improve your skills by trying them out for yourself. Many people find they need guidance with confronting and cathartic categories.

There are a number of blocks that occur in communication. One of the most common is misunderstanding. A lack of understanding, like many other blocks, can only be solved if you recognize it is operating.

How do you know when communication is not working? List the signs you look out for as listener and as a receiver. Listen and watch out for the alarm bells when you communicate.

IDENTIFY THE BLOCK

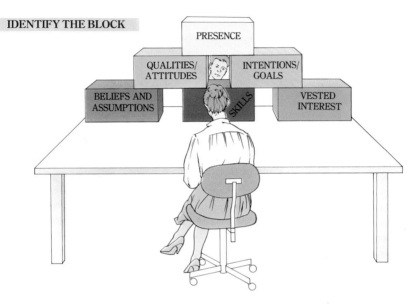

Once you recognize that communication is not working, try to identify where the problem is. It is often related to one of the following:

Presence
Are the people involved fully present for one another? If not, it might indicate that one or both of you do not really want to be communicating.

Qualities/attitudes
Do participants show respect, empathy, acceptance and understanding for each other? Indifference or hostility may reflect a deeper problem in the relationship.

Intentions/goals
Do people know what they want from the communication? Are they aware of each other's intentions or goals. Deception, a hidden agenda, ambiguity or double messages can ruin communication and possibly a trusting relationship.

Skills
Lack of good articulation in language, and inappropriateness in skill and strategy, are among the most common problems in communication. Saying what you mean and listening well can be difficult.

Beliefs and assumptions
You are continuously making aware and unaware assumptions about what people know, what you have told them and what they have understood. You also have beliefs about how people should behave.
When these beliefs are not fulfilled communication problems usually arise.

Vested interest
Almost everybody knows people with whom, for a variety of reasons, they would not be open and honest. Perhaps you are frightened that they might ridicule your vulnerabilities or would not be tolerant of your shortcomings. It may be that you avoid or are very formal with them.
Usually, you will find you are trying to control them or trying to protect yourself. Identifying what needs you are meeting by behaving in this way improves your communication.

BEHAVIOUR PATTERNS AS BLOCKS

There are certain kinds of behaviour which are the bane of good conversation. You may already be familiar with some of them, such as non-assertive behaviours and the behaviours of difficult people. The following behaviours also need to be avoided in communication.

★ REMEMBER!

Behaviours that block communication need to be handled skilfully. Watch out also for people who complain constantly, are always negative, overagreeable, or explode easily. The skills outlined in 'Difficult People' (pp. 124–133) and 'Getting Things Done' (pp. 112–123) will help you to handle them effectively.

The Know-it-all
Compensating for your feelings of inferiority by compulsively sharing real or imaginary knowledge or throwing cold water on another person's disclosure.

The Interrupter
Not really listening, formulating your next statement while the speaker is talking, and cutting in before the speaker has finished talking.

The Rambler
Talking to retain attention, to avoid it being obvious that you have nothing to say or have not made the effort to formulate statements. Statements are usually full of redundant words, which fill the void between empty or vague statements.

The Monologuist
Talking non-stop, speaking and listening to yourself, asking questions and answering them yourself, laughing at your own jokes even before you have finished telling them.

The Egotist
Compulsive 'I' statements serve mainly to evoke admiration for flagging self-esteem. Trying to force admiration from others only alienates.

Listening is more than just hearing. It means decoding language, interpreting nonverbal hidden messages, clarifying ambiguous ones and understanding other's point of view. It takes up more of your working hours than other activities.

People spend about 70 per cent of their working moments in communication, and listening makes up 45 per cent of that time.

Talking accounts, on average, for 30 per cent, reading 16 per cent and writing 9 per cent. In addition, many aspects of life depend largely on your ability to listen.

Listening is made up of four different sets of skills: attending, following and supporting, reflective listening and advanced listening. To become a better listener it is best to develop each skill area in turn.

WHY ARE PEOPLE POOR LISTENERS?

Most of us are not good listeners. Under normal circumstances, a whole host of factors interferes with listening well. Do any of the following apply to you?
● You are not trained to listen.
● You are not attending properly to those who are speaking.
● You get distracted.
● You often interfere with the listening process by making interpretations and judgements.
● You often interrupt.
● You are often preparing your reply while the speaker is talking.
● You often miss the real, deep or hidden meaning in the speaker's message.
● You often hear what you expect to hear rather than the intended message.

ATTENDING SKILLS

Underlying all the good listening skills is a healthy relationship, an attitude of real interest and openness to the speaker.

Attention can be communicated to another person if you adopt the following behaviours:

● Give primacy to the speaker's needs.
● Be open to what the speaker says, even if you disagree or lack interest.
● Lean toward the speaker with an open posture.
● Look at the speaker. Maintain appropriate eye contact.
● Create time and space for the speaker.
● Respond appropriately or relevantly.
● Notice your own and the speaker's verbal and nonverbal reactions, but do not get hooked by them.
● Avoid distractions.

FOLLOWING AND SUPPORTING

The most important task of the listener is to give speakers time and space to tell their story.

Following and supporting skills can be classified as:
● Door openers.
● Encouragers.
● Attentive silence.
● Open questions.
Door openers are invitations to talk. People often look as if they have something to communicate and the good listener can send a door opener to another person, using the following technique.
● Describe the other person's body language.
● Invite the person to talk.
● Maintain a silence. Give the person time to decide whether they want to respond.
● Attend. Adopt a posture of involvement, eye contact and body motion.

Encouragers are necessary to get the speaker to continue in full. They provide concrete evidence for the speaker that he is the focus of interest and attention.

Typically, encouragers are short, for example, 'Go on. . . I see. . .' and so on. Repeating one or two of the speaker's key words or the last word or two of a speaker's statement also helps encourage them.

TIME SPENT COMMUNICATING

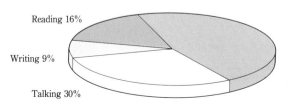

Reading 16%

Writing 9%

Talking 30%

Listening 45%

REFLECTIVE LISTENING

Silence on the part of the listener gives the speaker time to think about what he will say and how it will be said. It is one of the greatest aspects of good listening. Silence gives the listener the opportunity to attend and observe the speaker, and time to think about what the speaker is communicating.

Open questions provide an opportunity for the speaker to explore thoughts, feelings and experiences. They often take the form 'What. . .' or 'How. . .'

For instance, open questions could be 'What's on your mind?' 'How are you feeling about work?' These contrast with closed questions such as 'Are you unhappy?' 'Do you want to talk about work?' They usually have a yes, no or one word answer, and are used to focus in on something specific.

Attending and following skills are tremendously important in the listening process but the speaker needs to feel understood. You communicate understanding using the four reflective listening skills: paraphrasing, reflection of feeling, reflection of meaning, and summation reflection.

● Paraphrasing, or checking for understanding, focuses on the content of what the speaker has said. The listener makes a concise response to the speaker which states the heart of the speaker's content in the speaker's own words.

● Reflection of feeling involves mirroring back to the speaker the emotions which were experienced or are being experienced. For example, 'You felt furious' or 'It's really got you down'.

● Reflection of meaning is also known as basic empathy. Here the listener joins feelings and facts together in a succinct response. Often you can use a formula: 'You feel. . .because. . .' Whether or not you use the formula does not matter as long as you are able to indicate that you understood the person's feelings and what it was or is that caused them.

● Summative reflections are brief restatements of the main themes and feelings the speaker has expressed over a long period of conversation. They should help speakers organize their concerns and integrate the material. Often they can take the following form: 'It seems to be that you have looked at X, been involved with Y and in general avoided Z. You have felt pretty angry throughout.'

The preceding three areas of skills – if all used in combination – will transform your ability to listen and therefore your ability to understand. And that means you will be well on the way to communicating effectively because you will have a solid foundation upon which to base the way you relate to others.

However, you can advance your reflection skills by using the following guidelines:
● Do not fake understanding.
● Focus on the feelings and improve your sensitivity to feelings.
● Develop empathy in your voice – use tone and inflection to match the speaker's feeling state.
● Reflect concretely, not vaguely.
● Do not answer the speaker's questions, but try to reflect the feeling contained within the question.
● Do not tell the speaker you know how he feels – no one can ever fully know what it is like to be in another person's shoes.

★ REMEMBER!

If your mind starts wandering as you attend to a speaker you can say to yourself 'This is his time' to draw your attention back.

Since 85 per cent of our communication is nonverbal, attending to the nonverbal part of listening is fundamental.

Finally, remember that if you have really begun to get a sense of the speaker's world you can use responses which add to the speaker's understanding of himself and his problems. These additive responses should be used only to help the speaker enjoy a better insight into his situation, be better informed, take more reflective action or feel supported by the listener.

These responses build on what the speaker has stated, but through intuitive grasp of the direction in which the speaker is unfolding, goes a little further to accelerate the process.

During communication, you rely more on the message contained in the body language of the communicator than what is actually said, particularly if the two languages contradict each other. Your body, including posture, gesture and facial expression, is constantly sending messages to other people to make very powerful statements about who you are, how you are feeling and what you are thinking.

Body language, or nonverbal communication, can reinforce your verbal messages or it can discount them. It is often the basis on which people decide whether or not you are worth listening to. Sensitive communicators consciously make use of nonverbal aspects of behaviour or body language.

USING BODY LANGUAGE

You will probably have heard interesting messages which have been undermined by the speaker's having an irritating voice or a distracting idiosyncracy. To avoid this pitfall when speaking, use the following tips for the effective use of body language:
● Face the person. Do not be in direct opposition.
● Keep an open, receptive posture.
● Lean slightly toward the person.
● Place yourself close enough so you are both comfortable – not sitting behind desks.
● Take care with your appearance, however you choose to dress.
● Use contrast and variety in your voice and tone.
● Lower your voice for emphasis.
● Match the body language of the speaker without mimicking. This builds empathy.
● Avoid extremes of appearance unless your business is drawing attention to yourself.
● Show enthusiasm and sincerity.

There are other nonverbal channels of communication you should be aware of. Watch for these when you are communicating.
● Facial expression and facial movements, such as smiling, grimacing and frowning.
● Eye contact and eye quality, such as direct gaze.
● Your physical appearance, including your sex, age, body shape, hairstyle and clothing.
● Physical posture, such as open, closed, rigid, flexible or alert.
● Physical position and setting, your distance or closeness to person you are talking to.
● Movements and gestures, including whole body movements, illustrative gestures.
● Vocal quality and tone of voice, rate of speech, the volume and pitch of voice.

INTERPRETING BODY LANGUAGE

Even if you are not aware of it, you already know a great deal about body language. Most people are experienced at picking up the real message behind the words. However, the same signal may carry different meanings.

There are several ways of becoming more sensitive to the messages communicated by body language.
● Treat every element of body language as reflecting some statement made by the person. Sometimes this is obvious, as in a fashionable appearance. Sometimes it is very complex as in lack of eye contact.
● Look for clusters of signals. It is very difficult for a single element of body language to stand in isolation and mean one specific thing. But a cluster of signals may all combine to provide an underlying messsage.

HOW YOU COME ACROSS

There is one special technique that uses a video camera and monitor to explore the effect you make on others, particularly in relation to nonverbal communication. You need another person to help you with this.

● Sit in a chair facing the monitor, while your assistant focuses the video camera on you. The diagram illustrates the set-up you need.

● Your camera operator then invites you to talk about yourself for about four minutes. While this goes on, the focus of the camera should be slowly changed, including close-up and long shots, and shots that concentrate on particular areas of your face and body.

● While you are still looking at yourself on the monitor, have the other person gently ask the following questions. Does this person draw your attention?

Do you dislike what you hear? What are your feelings toward him or her?

Then think about what helps or hinders your message?

● Is your body language congruent with your message or does it distract from it?

● How you could improve your presentation?

At the end of the exercise replay the whole video and explore your feelings after the tape has been seen.

★ TEST YOURSELF!

If you cannot gain access to a video camera, try recording your voice, perhaps in front of a mirror, or talk about yourself to a friend who will give you feedback.

What do you notice? Use the same questions as if you were doing the exercise with the video camera.

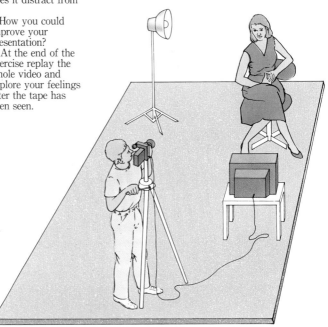

★ TRY THIS NOW!

Tune in to the various channels of body language from time to time to enhance your awareness and sensitivity. One good technique is to monitor one, two or a small group of people at a distance in a public place.

Write down what you see, how you feel about it, and your interpretation.

Do this exercise with a friend and see if your notes correspond. You will probably find that you noticed different aspects of body language and may

have even interpreted the same aspects differently. What do your findings tell you?

To practise interpretation, turn off the sound of a television set for 15 minutes each day just to watch all the nonverbal signals. Similarly, when you

are listening to a conversation try tuning out the words and just listen to the vocal qualities.

Practise communicating with a friend in a work situation and emphasize one channel of communication.

Reading is a complex activity. It means recognizing the words and decoding them, and extracting their meaning. It involves understanding the internal coherence of what is read, being able to link it with what you already know, and selecting and storing relevant information in your memory.

All these elements need to be carried out so that the information can be recalled, communicated and applied when required.

CHOOSING WHAT TO READ

Most busy people are faced with a considerable reading load on a daily or weekly basis. Most professionals and business people have to be ruthless in their selection of material.

Categorizing various written communications is one way of helping you deal with the pile. A simple tray system with labels such as 'urgent', 'soon', 'can wait', 'pass on' and 'throw away' will enable you to prioritize quickly.

It is best to do this as soon as you get a communication and have regular clearing out sessions.

You may also find it useful to sort out light material which can be read in short periods of time from those which need careful attention or need critical evaluation, memorizing or the formation of a response. You will need to set aside longer periods of time to read this latter type.

URGENT

SOON

CAN WAIT

PASS ON

THROW AWAY

WHY READ IT?

Besides sorting out what you are going to read, the next most important question to answer is why you want to read any given piece. Most people seem to read material without knowing why they are doing it and this results in grossly ineffective reading.

You can extract information more readily when you have prepared yourself to receive it, that is, amplified your interest or curiosity and clarified what you need to know or discover. What is the question you wish to answer by reading?

★ TRY THIS NOW!

You may be a skilled, but not fast, reader. To improve:
* *Be clear what you want from reading.*

* *Pull out the main points.*
* *Identify and vocalize the key words.*

★ TEST YOURSELF!

Do the following exercises for 15 minutes per day (one exercise per week) to improve your reading speed in one month. It will help to train your eyes in good reading reflexes and your mind to focus quickly on the key points in your material.

Use light novels to practise on difficult material. Highly skilled readers can read as quickly as they can turn the pages, with excellent comprehension.
* *Focus on groups of words rather than single words.*

* *Use a pencil to guide your eye along the line. Lift it upward and then back down to the next line in an easy rhythm.*
* *Using this movement, push yourself to read faster, doubling your rate each time. When you slow to decoding and extracting pace you will find you can do it faster.*
* *Push yourself to take in six lines, then a page at a time (in two seconds). Extract as many key words as you can, keeping to the time limit.*

READING SKILLS

Different types of purpose require different reading skills. For example, scanning helps you decide what to read further. Skimming can help you get an overview. Light reading will take you through easy material quickly, while in depth or word-for-word reading may be necessary for highly technical or complex new material.

Remember, you do not have to read everything just because it is written down. Be selective and do not feel guilty about skipping boring or useless information.

The following approach, devised by leading reading expert Tony Buzan, may be helpful.

Overview

● Read cover and flaps.
● Scan contents table.
● Read chapter heads, subheads, footnotes and graphs.
● Look at illustrations and photographs.
● Decide if you want to proceed.

Preview

● Read summary chapter or conclusion.
● Read chapter summaries.
● Read the beginnings and ends of chapters.
● Look for key words and phrases.

Inview

● Read sections previously unread.
● Skip difficult sections.
● Prepare for note-taking by marking in shorthand symbols important, essential and difficult passages.

Review

● Re-examine important sections.
● Make notes now, not earlier.
● Fill in any outstanding gaps left by earlier reading.
● Check notes for understanding and connections with existing knowledge.

Many people start at the beginning of a piece and plough steadily through the material, often frustrating themselves and retaining little. An intelligent reading strategy such as that mentioned above will greatly improve your capacity to decode and extract from even the most difficult material.

Remember, you decide what is important and worth retaining. Skilled reading is not an endurance test or a matter of sheer determination. It just takes practice to acquire the skills.

Speaking in public can take several forms, including lectures, speeches, debates or presentations. Each of these involves specialized techniques, but all demand that attention be paid to the basics.

Public speaking may be used to inform others of your ideas, to entertain them as in after-dinner speeches or celebrations, to persuade people toward your point of view or to undertake a course of action.

PREPARING A SPEECH

A speech will usually have a main purpose, and possibly a number of subgoals. It may be prepared or spontaneous. It needs to have an impact on the audience, maintain their interest and go a significant way toward meeting their main expectations.

A good way of preparing a speech is by:
● Choosing a topic that is appropriate to the setting and your audience.
● Limiting your speech to a single objective that fits your qualifications and experience.
● Researching to acquire the facts and other data you will use.
● Preparing an outline of your speech, which will serve as a summary of the points you want to make.

● Organizing the material you have gathered so that it maximizes the impact of your message.
● Writing the final form of the speech, making it as colourful and interesting as possible but reinforcing the central theme.
● Finally, delivering the speech to convey the message in a way that makes it easiest to receive and assimilate.

Know your audience
As in all communication knowing your audience is crucial. Are they expecting information, to be entertained, a sales pitch? What do they already know? What do they need to know?

What other assumptions about your audience can you make which will help you get your message across?

SHAPING THE MATERIAL

You must shape the material to make it easy for the audience to assimilate. This usually requires an introduction, followed by the main body of the material you wish to communicate, leading to a conclusion or summary of your main points.

There are a number of ways of organizing your information for maximum effect.

Topical
This requires that you divide the speech into various parts or topics and arrange them in the most effective order, dealing with each issue separately and linking them at the beginning and/or end. This format is useful for transmitting information.

Historical or time arrangement
This demands that information or experience is related in the natural sequence in which it occurred. Speeches which aim to teach or instruct might use this form of organization.

Spatial
This speech is structured in relation to the geographical location in which it is to take place or to which it refers. It might be used, for example, in a succession of places on a building site or in a museum.

Logical
This format is useful when presenting reasoned argument or proof. Each point proves the truth or provides a rationale for subsequent points. Deduction, proposition and other features of logical argument feature strongly.

Destroying the opposition
Also called residual reasoning, this is a means of structuring a speech where each solution to a problem is presented and shown to be ineffective or unsuitable. This process of elimination is carried on until you are left with one worthwhile solution – the one you are advocating.

Problem-solving
This form of presentation uses a problem-solving cycle to provide the sequence for information.

Oratory
This form of speech is primarily persuasive in nature and incites action or motivation. Points are arranged from the weakest to the strongest and are laden with strong emotional as well as rational appeal.

Personalize and supply
It will make your speech more memorable and effective if you can personalize it and support your ideas. Personalizing means sharing illustrative examples and anecdotes from your own experience. Some other ways of supporting are to:
- Provide statistics and research.
- Give factual data.
- Use exhibits.
- Include quotations.
- Provide expert testimony.
- Give comparisons and contrasts.
- Include audio-visual reports.

The introduction will need to attract the attention of your audience, prepare them for what is to come and help them understand the relevance of the material. Controversial statements, a challenge to the audience, a powerful but relevant quotation, a humourous incident are all good attention catchers.

DELIVERING THE SPEECH

Reading a speech from a script will no doubt cover what you want to say but it will probably be dull and monotonous. Public speaking needs to be full of expression and variation. The audience usually has a short attention span. The beginnings and ends of speeches are likely to be remembered so make sure these contain and repeat the most important information.

Use notes and phrases to prompt your speech. Vary your voice, pace, gestures and mode of presentation to keep the audience alert. People tend to forget most of what they hear, so use aids such as slides, models or video overhead projectors to aid memory and understanding during lengthy deliveries.

Emphasize key points with a pause, by lowering your voice and by movement and gesture. If you really need people to remember information provide a handout containing the text of what you have said.

★ REMEMBER!

To clarify what you want to say, ask yourself these questions.
- *What am I talking about?*
- *What is the message?*
- *What statement best conveys the message?*
- *What do I hope to achieve?*
- *Why am I giving the speech?*

To get things done effectively, and achieve satisfactory results, you must be able to progress from having ideas to taking action. This involves the appropriate use of available energy, and maintaining this energy and motivation over the time span taken to complete the task.

All tasks require some thought as well as action. And both of these require a range of personal skills. Bigger tasks, which involve enlisting the help of others, will demand a whole range of interpersonal skills, and possibly group coordination or leadership skills. Finally, getting things done involves mobilizing all those positive forces that help you to achieve your goals and also involves minimizing the effect of the unhelpful forces.

The following technique will enable you to get things done effectively. It has been adapted from the one used by the Coverdale Organisation, specialists in management consulting.

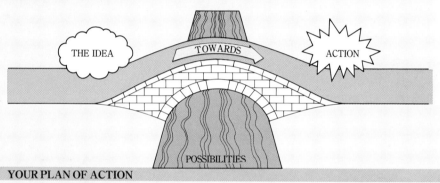

THE IDEA — TOWARDS — ACTION — POSSIBILITIES

YOUR PLAN OF ACTION

Your plan should be extremely specific and should spell out exactly who is going to do what, when and where it will be done, and how it is to be accomplished.

If you think this is unnecessary, remember that most New Year's resolutions almost always specify only what needs to be done, and almost equally invariably fail to make it to action. A proper plan is essential if you want to achieve the desired results.

Using your collection of internal colleagues, apply this process to a small straightforward task – buying an expensive present for a friend.

Dreaming
First, set the dreamer in you the task of visualizing the friend opening the present (see Direction setting pg. 116). Imagine the delight as he sees what you have given him. He is clearly touched by your thoughtful and appropriate gift. Notice what it is about the present which pleases your friend.

Gathering information
Now mobilize your information processor to gather together all the things you know about what your

THE DREAMER

THE INTUITOR AND THE LATERAL THINKER

THE INTERNAL COMMUNITY

To get major tasks done in the outer world it is common to organize people into roles or special functions, for example, leader, treasurer, etc. Equally it is beneficial to act as if, internally, you have similar roles or functional divisions within yourself, which you can draw on to achieve particular subtasks.

The divisions of your internal resources are sometimes called your internal colleagues or community. Using the right member of the community is essential for progress. These include:

● The dreamer, who creates the vision or the goal.
● The information processor, who collects together the data.
● The analyst, who breaks down the tasks into manageable steps and sequences.
● The planner, who decides who will do which tasks.
● The doer, who puts it into action.
● The reviewer, who helps boost performance by monitoring and giving constructive feedback.

THE KEY POINTS

When you are first attempting to move from ideas to action, you will need to evaluate a few key points in the process. You must determine your idea or vision, gather the necessary information, and then use this information to work out what needs to be done.

Your dreamer will help you to determine your vision or idea of what you want to achieve.

You then need to gather the information you require to arrive at a plan. For example, you must determine:

● What resources you need.
● What resources are available.
● Whose help you will need.
● Whose help is available.
● What are the options/possibilities.
● What are the risks attached to each option.

Then you must determine what has to be done. In this step you must identify all the subtasks which need to be completed to get you to the final result you want. These must then be put in order to determine what has to be done first.

friend likes and enjoys doing, and what talents he would like to develop. Try to remember particularly enjoyable things you have done together in the past, or presents he has given you which might provide clues to what he would like to have.

You may need to call on your intuitor or lateral thinker for their advice. They might take you away from material objects to things to share, such as tickets for a show.

You also need other kinds of information too, such as:

● How much money you can spend.
● How much time you can devote to looking for a present.
● How soon the event is, if relevant, such as a birthday or anniversary.

● What the effect will be if you opt for something rather unusual but it is not a success (the risk).
● Whether it would make sense to team up with someone else to get something together.

Analysing

When your information processor has collected and sifted through all this information, you should be in a position to decide what has to be done.

This is called analysing or first stage planning. Ask your analyser to map out the subtasks, in order. These might include:

● Deciding you need more information and will ask a mutual friend for it.
● Deciding on a choice of two possible presents, depending on which one you can get.

THE ACTIVE SELF CHECKS THE ORIGINAL VISION

UNLEASHING THE DOER

After you have developed and completed your plan of action, you will need to be able to review the process.

This will help you to learn from your experience, improve your performance, and determine which of your internal colleagues you can rely upon when carrying out a task on your own.

★ TRY THIS NOW!

Choose a relatively simple task to practise the ideas-to-action framework. Write down the heading of each section in turn. You may find you need to move backward and forward a bit.

Using the framework flexibly is fine, but you should always be able to identify which heading is right for where you are in the process.

DEGREE OF EFFECTIVENESS OF YOUR INTERNAL COLLEAGUES

Dreamer   Information processor

Intuitor

THE FINAL STAGES

After you have moved from ideas to action, you can then mobilize your planner to specify who is going to do which subtask when, where and how.

Finally, before you invite your doer to get the show on the road, just call back your dreamer to check how well your planner's plan relates to the dreamer's vision. If the dreamer is happy with the plan, then go ahead. If not, get your information processor to help you find out why not.

Now, unleash your doer and enjoy the satisfaction of having skilfully and appropriately brought all these aspects of yourself to bear to delight your friend.

REVIEWING

Reviewing involves looking back over what you have done and identifying which of your internal colleagues are particularly strong and effective, and do their share of the work fluently and easily.

It also involves looking at the ones who were not so strong, or who lacked confidence.

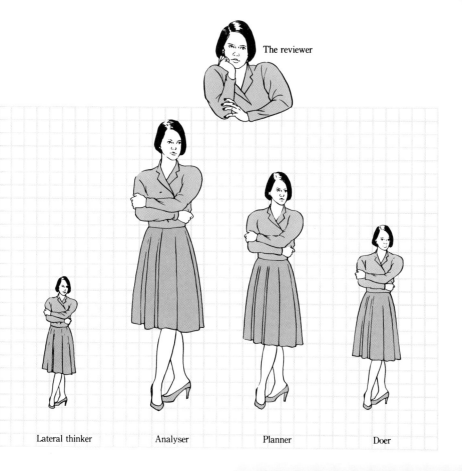

The reviewer

Lateral thinker   Analyser   Planner   Doer

Reviewing will help you to learn from the experience so that you can do it better, if necessary, next time.

Reviewing consists of:
• Checking to make sure that the final result was what you intended in the first place.
• Highlighting what was especially

successful and pinpointing the causes of the success.
• Noting any areas of difficulty and making plans to develop and improve them.

Getting your reviewer fit and active will do more for your whole internal team of colleagues than almost anything else.

★ THINGS THAT GO WRONG

When you are reviewing your plan, a number of things may go wrong.
• *You skip reviewing or do not spend enough time on this stage because you feel that the answers are obvious.*
• *You only focus on the successes and rationalize away the failures.*
• *You only focus on the failures and end*

up depressing yourself and your internal team. You fail to notice the things which actually work well and could be applied in future.
• *You theorize, speculate and generalize instead of getting down to the hard but valuable work of specifying in detail what happened and what the effects were.*

To get things done you need to determine what you are trying to achieve, that is, what your goals, aims and directions are. To do this, you will need to mobilize your dreamer. This member of your internal community is an extremely valuable one, particularly when getting things done, and is often accorded insufficient time and attention.

Your dreamer does not get on very well with your doer; each frustrates the other enormously. It is up to you to help them get on better terms, because they really need each other – and you really need them both. Managing these two internal colleagues is one of the key aspects of successful self management.

USING YOUR DREAMER

There are three main contributions your dreamer can make to getting things done. Your dreamer:
● Knows what you want in the future. Your dreamer can articulate what ideals, aims, purposes and objectives you would like to put your energy into achieving. It is your dreamer who knows what would give you satisfaction, what inspires you and what feels really worthwhile in terms of your values.
● Fashions a coherant picture of a future state or end product from half-formed thoughts. Your dreamer can symbolize and formulate your hopes and aspirations.
● Tells you what sort of level of achievement would count as success, and what standards are important to you, in reaching this goal.

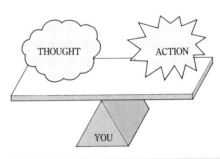

KNOWING WHERE YOU ARE GOING

To keep your dreamer functioning at peak form, and make the best use of its abilities, ask it these prompt questions each time you are considering taking action.

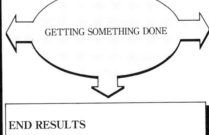

PURPOSES

● Why am I doing this task?
● What is it for? Who is it for?
● What benefit will I/ others get?

STANDARDS

● How will I know that my end result is satisfactory?
● How will I measure progress toward my purposes?
● What quantity/ quality am I going for?

END RESULTS

● What do I want to achieve?
● What will I end up with?
● What is my vision/ picture of the future?
● What will I have achieved in one week/three months?

AN EXAMPLE OF DIRECTION SETTING

To understand how your dreamer operates you should work through the following example. The task set is to make a presentation to someone important in your organization.

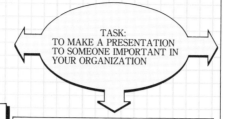

TASK:
TO MAKE A PRESENTATION TO SOMEONE IMPORTANT IN YOUR ORGANIZATION

PURPOSES

Why are you doing this task?
●To bring to their attention your achievements so far.
● To demonstrate that you are promotion material.
● To inform them of some key new developments which they need to take account of.

What are you doing this for?
It could be to convey some information to the other person.

What will the benefit be?
● To be adequately rewarded for your effort, or to get promoted.
● To benefit others so that they know about these new developments.
● To help the organization by staying ahead in a competitive market.

END RESULTS

What do you want to achieve/end up with? What is your vision?
● A 10-minute presentation drawing attention to three key developments, most of the time to be devoted to showing how and why these are crucial to the success of this organization, and the risks of ignoring them.
● A 20-minute presentation, giving figures and bar graphs, focusing in turn on each area in which you have made a significant contribution.
● A 30-minute presentation, divided into two halves of equal length. One half will be devoted to achievements so far, highlighting what is unique or

unusual about them. The other will outline ideas for future development, particularly areas in which you think your specific skills would make an impact, and show the potential you have which the organization is not currently using.

What will you have within a set time period?
● An impressed recipient, who is just a little worried that if you do not get a pay rise you may take your talents elsewhere.
● An impressed recipient who can see how you could/would operate given scope.
● A better informed recipient who is in a position to ensure the continued success of the organization.

STANDARDS

How will you know your end result is satisfactory?
● If within three months you get a rise of at least 10 per cent (quantity).
● If within six months you are promoted into X or Y role (quality).
● If within six months decisions are actually taken which will give your company the edge over your competitors (quality).

How will you measure progress?
● Within a week you will have a date for your presentation. Within two weeks you will have completed the preparation work.
● If within one month after your presentation you hear that the recipient has been thoughtfully discussing the points you have made with others whom he/she respects.
● If within three months you hear on the grapevine that you are being considered for promotion.

★ REMEMBER!

● *Purposes always start with 'In order to . . .' or 'So as to be able to . . .'*
● *Answers to the question why?, which start with 'because',*

give you information which will be very useful to your internal information processor. They do not set direction. They push you. It is your

dreamer that pulls you into the future.
● *Analysing past mistakes is not as helpful as you might think. The analysis may be correct, but*

what it certainly will be is partial or incomplete, and damaging to your confidence and willingness to take risks and try things.

To get things done effectively and efficiently, you will need to enlist cooperation from other people as well as from your internal colleagues. There is a variety of methods and approaches you can use to achieve your goals, some more effective than others.

Your approach can be assertive, submissive, aggressive or indirect, depending on how you are feeling about yourself and the situation at hand. You are likely to fall into an aggressive, submissive or indirect approach when you are feeling least secure and confident in yourself.

THE AGGRESSIVE APPROACH

Just do it!

THE SUBMISSIVE APPROACH

I'll agree to anything.

When you are being aggressive, you demand that your priorities are met without allowing others to state theirs, and without taking them into account. You bulldoze or give them orders when a request would be more appropriate.

You insist that things are done exactly as you would do them, and do not allow other people to adopt their own style.

When you are being aggressive you do not give positive feedback unless it cannot be avoided; then you counteract it immediately with non-constructive criticism. You are readily critical and overreact, attacking the person's personality, labelling them negatively or blaming them. You may set out to hurt them in their vulnerable areas.

The effects

If you use the aggressive approach:
● You sometimes achieve short-term results because other people might allow themselves to be bulldozed.
● In the long term, there may be a lack of cooperation. Others are more likely to feel a lack of motivation or feel aggrieved, and may sabotage your efforts behind the scenes.
● The work may get done badly or be late. Others may immediately retaliate in a reciprocally aggressive manner.

You may not be taken seriously if you are seen as being too hard-hitting, when in fact you have some valid points to make underneath all your bluster.
● People will avoid you.

When you are being submissive, you hold back from stating what you want done, perhaps to avoid taking a high profile leadership role, or so that you will be liked. You hope that others will just get on with the job at hand without much guidance from you.

You give little feedback, and you let embarrassment stop you from paying compliments. You underreact when others are not doing their job, beating around the bush and not letting them know what you think.

You might not let your feelings and impressions be known at all, so that the other person assumes they have your approval, or fails to take you into account because they do not realize their effect on you.

The effects

If you use a submissive approach:
● In the short term, others might think how nice and cooperative you are.
● Others show you scant consideration, since they feel they do not need to take you into account.
● You may fall victim to becoming overloaded with tasks which are not your responsibility, so that you do not have the time or energy to deal effectively with your own work.
● You may end up bringing out the aggressive tendencies in others by persistent submissiveness.

★ REMEMBER!

To get things done with a team depends on the relationship you build up with its members. An assertive approach is the most effective in the long term.

Some of the non-assertive approaches may work, and may suit the situation in the short term, but they have damaging consequences on cooperation in the future. You may find that you accomplish your aims and the tasks, but at the expense of your relationship with the others involved.

THE INDIRECT APPROACH

You're smart. You'll agree with me.

This involves getting another person to comply by means of insincere flattery, bulldozing with a veneer of friendliness, indirect threat, emotional blackmail, flirtation, sarcasm or hinting. You might try to persuade others to think or do things your way as if it were their idea, or by citing a policy or orders from elsewhere (sometimes fictitious).

You give compliments to get your own way by ego-boosting first. Verbal examples of indirect aggression can include jokey put-downs and sarcasm. Non-verbal indirect criticisms include turning your eyes upward, raising your eyebrows, shrugging your shoulders or sighing, perhaps so others present can see you, but the object of your criticism cannot. There could also be a critical silence.

Sending critical messages via someone else might be an indirect way of abusing both the object of the criticism and also the messenger, since the bearer of second-hand criticism is often the one who receives the retaliation.

The effects
If you use the indirect approach:
● You may find it is often the most effective way of getting what you want from someone, as long as you are only concerned with short-term results.
● In the long term, people realize that they are being manipulated. They may retaliate indirectly or aggressively, or mistrust or avoid you in the future.

The most effective method to use when trying to accomplish your goal is the assertive approach. This includes letting other people know what your priorities, preferences, wants or needs are in a specific situation, while allowing them to state theirs and taking them into account.

When you are being assertive you state these needs or make your requests with an appropriate strength of feeling, which indicates the extent to which they are important to you. When your statement or request is not being acknowledged or acted on sufficiently, and it is important, then you persist.

Assertiveness can come naturally when you are feeling realistically self-confident. When you are under stress, your internal equilibrium can be shaken and it is easier to move into one of the other, non-assertive approaches.

BODY POSTURE

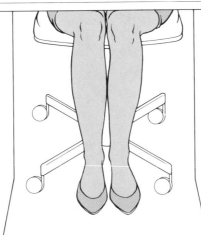

When you are aiming to be assertive, take notice of your body posture. This nonverbal method of communication can say a lot about how you are feeling, and tell the other person things about which you are not even aware. When being assertive keep your body relaxed and upright.

Pay attention to which part of your body tenses or collapses when you are in one of the non-assertive approaches.

In particular, check your back, arms, hands and shoulders. Also notice the tone in your voice, and what your face and head feel like.

If you find that you are tense and nervous, you should learn to relax. There are a number of different relaxation techniques (see pp. 86–87) that can help you. And merely adjusting your body position can help you regain more of your internal equilibrium.

THE EFFECTS OF THE ASSERTIVE APPROACH

When dealing with other people in trying to accomplish certain tasks, you will undoubtedly find that the assertive approach is the most effective. You will find that you are more likely to get the cooperation of others in getting things done, since they respect you and feel respected by you.

However, success does not only have to be defined by getting exactly what you want from others in a given situation. Another means of success is not getting exactly what you want done on one particular occasion, but achieving cooperation from the other person or persons involved in the future. Success can also be feeling better about yourself for having dealt with a situation in a way that retains your self-respect and does not put others down.

I'M OKAY
YOU'RE OKAY

RESPECTING INDIVIDUAL RIGHTS

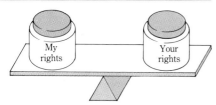

My rights

Your rights

When you are being assertive, always remember to take account of your rights, and the rights of the people you are dealing with. These can be both general and specific.

General rights
Everyone has a right to:
● Express themselves, provided they do not set out to hurt others or put others down in the process.
● Be treated with respect as intelligent, capable and equal human beings.
● State their own needs and priorities as an individual, whatever other people expect of them because of their roles in life.
● Deal with people without having to like or approve of them.

Specific rights
Everyone has a right to:
● Express their opinions and values.
● Express their emotions when they decide the right time and place to do so.
● Ask for what they want.
● Say yes or no for themselves.
● Be fallible.
● Change their minds.
● Say they do not understand.
● Decide for themselves whether or not they are responsible for finding a solution to another person's problem.

★ **REMEMBER!**

There are three key points to bear in mind when you are using the assertive approach to get things done. These are:
● *Body posture, which should be relaxed and upright.*
● *Respecting your own and other people's rights as individuals.*
● *Being verbally direct and specific, and persisting if your request is important.*

As well as the nonverbal clues you use when being assertive, there are a number of verbal keys that you can use to be successful. These include being able to get and keep a person's attention, and being able to state clearly what you want.

You must first decide exactly what you want done. At times you may find that it is easier to specify what it is you do not want, but going about it in this manner is negative and not as effective. You need to be able to express the positive side of what you want.

CHECKLIST FOR VERBAL ASSERTIVENESS

When being verbally assertive:
● Decide exactly what you want done.
● Get the person's attention.
● Say what you want concisely.
● Listen.
● Be persistent.
● Spell out the consequences.
● Confirm the agreement.
● Give feedback.

To make assertive statements:
● Make 'I' statements that are brief and to the point.
● Make a distinction between fact and opinion.
● Make suggestions without using 'should' and 'ought'.
● Criticize constructively and avoid blaming.
● Seek out others'

opinions.
● Be willing to explore other solutions.

BEING VERBALLY ASSERTIVE

Once you have determined what precisely it is that you are looking for, the next step is to get the person's attention. There is no point in telling someone what you want done if they are not able to hear you and take in what you are saying.

When you are deciding to discuss a matter with someone, take into account the following:
● The environment, such as where you

are, how many other people are around, if your message can be heard without strain, the amount of noise in the area.
● Your physical distance from the person you are addressing.
● Whether the person is concentrating on something else. If so, be sure to give them a chance to realize that you want to talk to them by using their name, touching their arm, or telling them you want to say something.

Say what you want
Then you must make a clear statement of exactly what you want the other person to do. This statement needs to have at least a 'you' in it, and possibly an 'I'. For example 'I would like you to . . .' or 'Would you . . .'

When making the statement, show the appropriate strength of feeling and indicate the level of priority.

If every request that you make is expressed as an

urgent priority, other people will think you are crying wolf and will not take you seriously.

Then you must wait, and listen for their response. You might find you are willing to negotiate when you hear further information.

When you have come to an agreement you should confirm it in writing. This clarifies any misunderstandings and gives a clear basis for feedback.

BE PERSISTENT

If you have not received a satisfactory answer, and the issue is still important to you, you need to persist. There are two methods for doing so.
• The first is called 'broken record'. This involves repeating your request statement over and over until it is heard properly. This method is particularly useful when someone does not take in what you have said or uses diversionary tactics. Maintain your tone of voice, keeping it at the same volume rather than escalating into pleading or exasperation.
• The second method is 'reflecting the response'. You first must prove that you have listened. To say 'I take your point', or 'I hear what you say' may not be enough. Instead, summarize what the other person has said, preferably repeating their key words. Alternatively, you could reply to any relevant questions. Second, repeat your request statement to reinforce how important it is to you.

If neither of these methods is successful you may find it appropriate to spell out the positive consequences that would occur if your request is met. Or you may need to spell out the consequences that would result from a lack of cooperation.

GIVING FEEDBACK

You may find yourself in situations in which you must provide feedback to other people. This can be positive feedback, if the task is done well, or it may be constructive criticism, if you are trying to improve the performance of another person and get them to do what is asked or needed.

You should balance the two types of feedback if you are dealing with someone on a long-term basis. If you are always full of praise, they may be suspicious or become oblivious to what you are saying. If you are only critical, then the other person may become demoralized and resentful. Do not search around for something to balance each compliment or criticism. Let each one stand on its own.

Positive feedback
When your request has been met, provide the other person with positive feedback to show genuine appreciation. When giving feedback, comment specifically on their actions, including what was done and how it was accomplished.

Persist with your compliment if it gets thrown back in your face by someone who is embarrassed or suspicious. Ask the recipient simply to accept your compliment. Then repeat your positive statement.

Constructive criticism
If you find that a person is not doing what you asked, you may need to give constructive criticism. This is hard to give, and often hard to take. When giving constructive criticism, go straight to the point, commenting on the person's behaviour, not their personality.

Speak for yourself and state how the behaviour affected you. Say what type of behaviour you prefer as an alternative.

Give the other person a chance to respond. Listen to what they have to say. Persist in your criticism if no further information comes to light to lead you to change your mind.

WHEN ASSERTIVENESS DOES NOT WORK

If you feel that you are not able to get things done, in spite of being assertive, consider the following.
• Have you really been assertive? Check that your approach fits the assertive category fully. If not, try again using a more assertive approach. It is often possible to retrieve an unpromising situation.
• Apologize if you have made a mistake in your approach. Keep your apology assertive by being specific about exactly what you did that you regret, and by only saying it once.
• Consider what compromise you would be willing to make.
• Be prepared to let go and drop your request if no compromise can be reached.
• Consider your priorities in dealing with the person involved. For example, in a long-term relationship, there may be other important areas of cooperation you might require in the future. Being seen to genuinely maintain your respect of their rights and your own, will stand you in good stead for future negotiations.

WHAT IS A DIFFICULT PERSON?

Difficult people are characters you may encounter in all kinds of situations. These are the people about whom you may receive warning signals and statements from others who have dealt with them. These warnings are intended to alert you to potential snags you may have in coping with these difficult characters as a result of their unpleasant or unsociable behaviour.

If, however, you press for an explanation of what it is that is difficult about the person in question, the reply you get will probably be a mixture of feeling, reaction, judgement and a description of problematic behaviour. What you may find if you are familiar with this 'difficult person' is that you agree with some of the information, but not with other aspects of it.

CAUSES OF DIFFICULT BEHAVIOUR

In reality, there are no 'difficult people', since it is not the person who is difficult but the behaviour of that person. The problem is actually one of communication or cooperation between the two parties involved, and is usually sparked off or triggered by some idiosyncratic behaviour on the part of the difficult person.

Problems may arise because of assumptions about what the other person knows, a disagreement about factual information, or a refusal to make a satisfying contract.

Difficult behaviour may be interpreted as sheer stubbornness, but in reality may be an expression of fear or anxiety on the part of the other person. The difficulty may also be caused by a conflict over values, or a difference in personality type.

Separating the problematic values, attitudes and behaviour patterns from the person manifesting them will enable you to cope with the behaviour while, at the same time, being supportive to the person in question.

IDENTIFYING THE DIFFICULT PERSON

The fairy tale *The Pied Piper of Hamelin* illustrates the danger you run if you fail to deal constructively with difficult people. It also provides a useful map for categorizing certain types of problematic behaviour.

The people of Hamelin were living happily until they are plagued by rats, the oppressors. The helpless villagers are the victims, while the Pied Piper is the rescuer who, after leading the rats to destruction, returns to collect payment. The villagers refuse, so the Piper plays his whistle and leads the children away from the village.

The Pied Piper is first the rescuer, then the victim when the villagers do not pay him. But he becomes an oppressor when he leads the children away.

The oppressor is undoubtedly a difficult person to deal with. However, the oppressor may also be both rescuer and victim at other times. The rescuer is rarely seen as a difficult person. But there is always a price to be paid for dependency, and people are often resentful or not prepared to pay the price of being rescued when it becomes due.

The victim is also rarely seen as a difficult person. But in this example the villager's inability to deal with the rats, that is, their lack of autonomy, caused them to accept the Piper's help. They thus become dependent.

It is this dependency that causes problems and leads to refusal to pay the price of rescue. So the villagers themselves become oppressed by the Pied Piper.

Even seemingly powerless victims are not always what they appear to be, and can often be experienced as aggressive when unappropriately dependent.

★ REMEMBER!

● *Being a victim (that is, not taking responsibility for yourself) will attract oppressors. Paradoxically, these may often appear as rescuers in the first instance.*

● *Being a compulsive rescuer does nobody a favour, least of all yourself. And what will be the price you demand in return?*

● *Oppressors should look at how they themselves have been oppressed before they 'do unto others what has been done to them' – even in the name of helping.*

WHO ARE YOUR DIFFICULT PEOPLE?

Racist

Doesn't respect my rights

Sexist

Uncooperative

Puts me down

Incompetent

Insensitive

Deceitful

Gives double messages

Doesn't give
straight answers

Think for a moment about what the phrase 'difficult people' means to you. Initially, you may define a difficult person as one who is insensitive, deceitful, sexist, racist or uncooperative. You might say difficult people are those who do not respect your rights, who give you double messages or who criticize you. If this is the case, notice that you have been focusing on the other person and not on yourself.

Now imagine yourself in situations in which various people created difficulty for you. Notice what the person's behaviour, attitude and tone was. How did you respond to it? For example: How did you feel? What did you think? How did you behave toward that person? Give yourself some time to ponder a few similar situations. Do you notice any patterns that are emerging?

In the first part of the exercise, there is likely to be a great deal of similarity in the labels and the behaviour that people deem as being difficult. However, there is likely to be a wide range of response to the second part of the exercise. This is because there seems to be significant agreement in our culture as to what asocial or troublesome behaviour is, but there is not the same shared response or skill in dealing with such behaviour.

When dealing with difficult people, each person's response will vary greatly, from avoidance or attack to being kind and supportive.

Everyone will be bothered by some people, some kinds of behaviour, in some situations, and at certain times that might not create difficulty for others.

★ TEST YOURSELF!

It is important to learn to create categories for the various kinds of people you think are difficult. This will help you to manage their effect on you, and to choose an appropriate strategy to deal with them.
● Reflect on the people you find difficult and write down their names. Visualize each person, including their behaviour, the setting
in which the behaviour occurs, their attitude and their speech.
● Note how the behaviour affects you. What are your thoughts, your feelings and your own behaviour with regard to this person?
● How do you respond to each person and each behaviour? Is it avoidance, attack, sarcasm, anxiety?
● Do you notice any patterns emerging regarding the kind of person you find difficult, their specific behaviour and the settings? Does your response vary? What do you find useful in this information?
● Now repeat the exercise, but from another person's perspective. Who finds you difficult? What do they find difficult about you?
How does it affect them? How do they respond?
● Was it easier to define your difficult people or to define what people find difficult about you? Was there similarity or overlap in the answers to both? You can check the answers with the people involved if you wish to have more reliable information.

Creating categories for certain types of difficult behaviour will help you to understand the people involved. It will also help you decide how best to deal with them. You should learn to distinguish between the troublesome behaviour itself and the person exhibiting that behaviour; such a distinction will help you to empathize with the person while rejecting the behaviour, or at least finding it disagreeable.

Remember, also, that these categories are only labels. They do not represent the totality of the person's behaviour. They are merely a way of viewing behaviour and of discriminating between behaviours to enable a more appropriate response.

TYPES OF DIFFICULT BEHAVIOUR

The following descriptions of various types of difficult behaviour are intended to help you understand difficult people better. These types of behaviour are essentially defensive, self-protective or compensatory. You need to look behind them to see the real needs of the person.

As you begin to understand the behaviour of others you may also understand and accept yourself. Understanding and empathizing are essential first steps in any constructive strategy for dealing with difficult people.

These categories are a useful way of identifying different types of behaviour. They are caricatures or stereotypes, and no person will fit into any of the categories completely.

You will recognize aspects of yourself in each of them. You will find that you behave in one way with one person or in one situation, and in another with a different person.

In addition to the five difficult

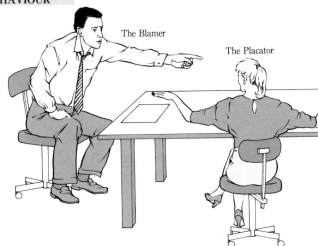

The Blamer

The Placator

characters outlined below there is another important type of person. This is the leveller, the person who has a positive way of relating to others. He is straight talking, and does not manipulate, play the victim or interfere unasked.

Levellers will usually speak only for themselves, and they will speak directly to you. There will be a consistency between what they say and what they do, and between what they say and how they say it.

The Blamer

The blamer judges, bullies, disagrees, compares, and complains. He sees himself as the boss, even a dictator. He comes across as loud, tense, tyrannical, and often wags or points his index finger accusingly. In reality, the blamer feels lonely and insignificant, and behind all the appearance of strength craves success but rarely acknowledges it.

The Placator

The placator pacifies, smoothes over differences, agrees with everything, covers up and defends gently. He sees himself as the peacemaker and helper. He comes across as ingratiating, powerless, helpless, and almost too good to be true. The placator really feels worthless inside and constantly needs approval and somebody to fuse with or depend on to make him feel secure.

★ TRY THIS NOW!

To explore these stereotypes, see if you can form a clear image of each of the five categories of difficult behaviour, including body posture, voice and attitude.

● *Are some more familiar to you than others? Try to amplify the stereotypes by adding aspects of your own behaviour.*

● *Visualize again the difficult people in your life. Do any of the categories apply to them? Amplify your findings using the person's words and behaviour. What do you discover about them as you imitate their behaviour in this way?*

This exercise should help you to gain perspective on what the other person may be doing.

The Computer

The Avoider

The Distractor

The Computer

The computer lectures objectively, calculates, uses logic and interprets. He thinks of himself as the archetype of objectivity. He comes across as unfeeling, disassociated, distant and dry. He often uses long words in a patronizing way, giving the impression of being calm and collected. Inside, the computer feels terribly vulnerable and is threatened by intimacy and feeling, while at the same time longing for it.

The Distracter

The distracter makes irrelevant statements, rarely responds to points made, and performs many tasks at once. He comes across as scatty, childish and ungrounded, which can make you feel unsettled or confused. Deep down this person has an unacknowledged and chronic need for attention and caring. He also has a sense of purposelessness about his life and does not feel that he belongs anywhere.

The Avoider

The avoider circulates quietly, pretends not to understand, makes excuses, plays absentminded or forgetful, or looks away. He thinks he is superior to others in many ways. He comes across as weak or reticent, and often incoherent. Internally this person is frightened of the world. He often wishes that somebody would care enough to tie him down with supportive challenges and physical nurture.

OTHER CATEGORIES OF BEHAVIOUR

There is another way of categorizing difficult people, which distinguishes between aggressive, submissive, indirect and assertive stereotypes (see Getting Things Done pp.118–123). You may find that you prefer to use this particular method of categorizing difficult people rather than the one above.

The aggressive person violates the rights of others and achieves goals at their expense. He uses humiliation and deprecation to achieve his goals.

The submissive person allows others to choose for him. He allows his rights to be violated and allows others to take advantage of him.

The indirect person causes others to feel betrayed. He deceives others and engages in concealed attacks.

The assertive person is similar to the leveller. He takes responsibility for his own actions, protects his own rights and respects those of others. He is direct and honest.

Almost invariably any of the categories of behaviour described on the previous pages have the effect of lowering your self-esteem. They may hit the tender areas in your self-image and paralyse your ability to respond appropriately. When confronted with difficult behaviour you may feel hurt, devalued, frustrated or rejected. It is also common to feel confused and unable to realize precisely what is going on. You may only be aware that you are having an unpleasant or distasteful experience.

POWER AND DIFFICULT BEHAVIOUR

So many of the problems that arise with difficult people stem from the fact you may feel powerless in the face of such people.

People learn powerlessness, or helplessness as it is often called, in response to situations in which they see no connection between what happens to them and their own actions. This response can be unlearned by appreciating that your thoughts and actions do influence people and the outcome of dealing with them in most situations.

In dealing with difficult people you probably have the sense of being controlled in some way. If you give in to this experience, and begin to believe that you are at the mercy of such people, you render yourself powerless.

By believing and acting as if you can decide, as if you have choices, then you can respond in a variety of ways. Staying in touch with your own centre of direction is fundamental in dealing with difficult people.

Failure, in itself, does not result in such feelings of powerlessness. But chronic and persistent failure will make you believe you are helpless. Opportunities for you to take charge of your life and to experience positive outcome from your actions will increase control from within and reduce 'learned helplessness'.

THE IMPORTANCE OF CHOICE

As a child, most decisions are made for you. You are told what to do, how to do it, what to learn, and how to behave. Therefore, it is not surprising that you learn to believe that you are controlled from the outside and that you are not responsible for your own behaviour.

As you get older, you have more opportunity to make your own decisions and choices. Often, however, many people do not take advantage of these opportunities and behave as if they did not exist.

To become self-empowered, which is the opposite of being in a state of learned helplessness, it is essential that you begin to believe that you can make your own decisions and choices, and that you also behave as if this were true.

Achieving this is described as reaching the point of control or choice. When individuals experience control as being within themselves rather than external they:
● Accept more responsibility for their own behaviour.
● See other people as being more responsible for their own behaviour.
● Notice more of what is happening around them.
● Are less anxious.
● Are less coercive when given power.
● Prefer activities involving skill to those involving chance.
● Have greater self-control or choice in their behaviour.

★ TEST YOURSELF!

Try this to discover how difficult people affect you and help you to determine what is the best strategy in various situations.

When you encounter a difficult person, do you feel;
● *Invaded or attacked?*
● *Rejected, deprived or ignored?*
● *Engaged in dialogue?*

As you meet various people throughout the day, notice whether any of the three experiences reflects the dominant pattern in your relationship with them. Are you happy with your findings? How could you improve things?

Did you notice any pattern of response with difficult people? What caused the pattern or the specific response to each person? Could you inhibit the response in favour of another, assuming it was unconstructive? What other ways could you respond if you encountered this type of situation again? Also remember when you handled similar situations well. What was different, and what did you do then?

RESPONSES TO DIFFICULT BEHAVIOUR

As well as defining the types of difficult people, it is useful to have some way of quickly categorizing your own response to their various behaviours. There are a number of responses you may have, and the following quick – but effective – measures may help you identify your reaction.

When dealing with each other, people move toward, away from, or against one another. When you are in a situation with another person, you should ask yourself these questions:

● Do I feel attacked by this person and/or have they invaded my physical or psychological space?
● Do I feel rejected and/or deprived? Have they taken flight/absented themselves from me or the situation?
● Do I feel met and recognized and/or

that I am in dialogue with this person?

If you feel invaded or persistently attacked you may take flight or withdraw. On the other hand, if you feel rejected or deprived you may tend to talk, pursue or manipulate. None of these options is likely to be successful in the long term.

The most effective response to difficult people lies in dialogue, or in levelling or assertive behaviour. Dialogue means respecting the views, desires, and feelings of others. It involves saying what you want, listening to the other person to learn about his experience, finding a common language to talk in, and doing something together that could resolve the conflict or frustration.

Levelling involves straight talking, giving the same message with your

voice and body as you do with your words. When you level you criticize or evaluate the behaviour, not the person. You apologize for an unintentional act, not your existence. You say you want to change the subject instead of engaging in disruptive distraction.

Assertive behaviour is standing up for your rights and respecting the rights of others. It involves stating clearly what you want from the other person, but not trying to win at all costs.

Choosing your response

Most of us tend to select people and situations that make us feel good and avoid those which we do not handle competently. But there will be times when you have to deal with people you

might ordinarily steer clear of. Even in these situations it is essential to remember that you have choices about how you respond to people.

The usefulness of the following options will depend on the situation and the other person. You will need to work out a process for choosing the appropriate strategy, using the information you have acquired to date.

Remember there is no right way to deal with difficult people. There are many ways, all of which will work. Most important is to discover what works for you. You can:
● Ignore the behaviour.
● Allow yourself to be overwhelmed by it/accept it.
● Respond in kind.
● Stand firm and declare your boundaries and limits.
● Yield/let go.
● Acknowledge and tolerate the behaviour, and then move on.
● Change/adapt yourself to the behaviour.
● Try to influence the other person to change.
● Pull rank or get the system to pressure the other person.
● Delay your reaction to play for time.
● Define the situation as a shared problem and make a contract to solve it.
● Ask a friend for help in relating to the difficult person.

Stay relaxed and centred

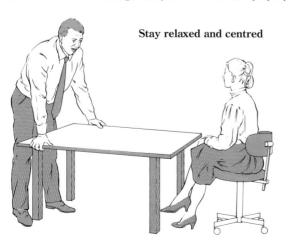

Many people are afraid to take a more active approach when confronted by difficult people. They may be fearful that they will not handle it correctly.

When you are dealing with difficult people, there are a number of steps you can take. You may find parts of this process cumbersome. Do not worry if at first you are unable to manage the whole process. Concentrate on one part at a time and then combine them.

Like any worthwhile skill it will take time to perfect. Be sure to notice the parts you do well already and build on these. In the first instance you will have to go through the initial stages before you interact with the person, but as you become more familiar with the process and integrate the skills you will be more able to respond spontaneously and appropriately.

DEALING WITH DIFFICULT PEOPLE

- Recognize and acknowledge how you are feeling. You do not have to express this or act on it.
- Stop and play for time, if necessary. You do not have to respond immediately. Do not be forced into a destructive response by your own compulsion to act or from outside pressure.
- Take the attitude that it is ignorance and inability rather than intention on the part of the difficult person.
- Control your response by self-management. Do not get taken in by their behaviour and overreact.
- Determine your values and goals. Work out what you need to get from the situation and how important it is to you.
- Label the person's behaviour. Decide how to deal with it, using the options above.
- Implement your strategy.

USEFUL SKILLS

There are a number of skills you will find useful in dealing with difficult behaviour.

Basic assertion
- Briefly state what you need or want, your belief or opinion. Be as specific as possible.

Broken record
- Repeat your statement using the same tone of voice and volume each time. 'I appreciate that you are busy but I need . . .'

Self disclosure
- State how a behaviour affects you, or state how you are feeling before making a request or confronting. 'I feel anxious saying this but I want you to know . . .'

Compromising
- Having asked for what you really need be prepared to compromise where there is a genuine clash of needs.

Catharsis
- If you are too angry or too frightened to deal with the person or behaviour, release your anger or fear with a friend or on your own. For example, you might beat a cushion with a tennis racquet and shout or scream to release your anger.

Control of feelings
- Switch attention away from what is generating your feelings. For example, you might count backward from 100 leaving out every second odd number.

Check for understanding
- Using your own words, paraphrase what the other person has said and ask if they feel you got the message.

Negative inquiry
- Use this skill where you have given negative criticism and a person has indicated a desire to give you feedback. 'You have heard what I have to say, is there anything you want to say to me?'

Interpreting
- Say what you think is going on at a process level, which may be causing the difficulty between you. 'I think you are annoyed with me and are not saying so.'

Giving feedback
- Positive feedback involves stating briefly what you liked or appreciated. Be spontaneous and honest. When giving negative feedback you should go straight to the point once you have checked that the person is willing to receive it.

Conflict resolution
- Where there is conflict which has not yet been brought to the surface, you can try two skills in succession. First polarize positions so the conflicting needs are recognized and stated. Then you can seek a compromise that recognizes the dignity and needs of both parties.

USING CONFRONTATION

When most people think of confrontation they think of a head-on collision between opponents. This is not what is required when dealing with difficult behaviour.

Successful confrontation is a skill few people are taught. Most will either avoid the issue by beating around the bush or be too heavy-handed. The result of these tactics is that the person may either be confused, or be so devastated by the onslaught that the confrontation is of little constructive use to anybody.

The aim of constructive confrontation is 'to tell the truth lovingly'. It can have two results. It can help you get what you want, or it can help the other person to learn and grow.

TO ACHIEVE YOUR GOALS
If the point of the confrontation is to achieve what you want:
● First clearly state the person's behaviour. 'You always walk off in the middle of an argument'.
● Then state the effect the person's behaviour has on you. 'I feel rejected and I get really furious with you.'
● Refer to a recent

incident as an example of the behaviour. 'For example, this happened last night when we differed over who was meant to be checking the work sheets.'
● Demand the change that is required. 'Well, in future I would like you to stay until we finish the argument or we both agree to leave it until another time.'

TO HELP OTHERS GROW
To use confrontation to enable others to develop and grow:
● First make a contract. For example, you might ask the difficult person 'Are you willing to hear some feedback?'
● Then identify the issue. 'I would like to talk about the effect of your behaviour on myself and others.'
● State the problem behaviour clearly. 'You continually pass remarks that many, including myself, find hurtful and alienating.'
● Explain the relevance to the person. 'If your behaviour continues it is likely to result in your being rejected by the team, or in others leaving unnecessarily.'
● Allow time and space for the person to react and respond. They will need supportive attention.

Styles of confrontation

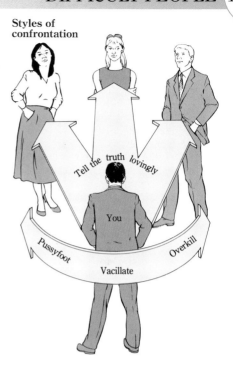

Tell the truth lovingly

You

Pussyfoot

Vacillate

Overkill

★ REMEMBER!

Even though it is direct and loving, confrontation will inevitably cause discomfort or even mild shock in the person toward whom it is directed. You will need to allow for this and adopt a supportive attitude. Hold your ground, be willing to listen and clarify your confrontation, if required. When practising constructive confrontation:
● *Choose a time when the person is most open to hearing you.*

● *Choose a place where you will not be interrupted.*
● *If it does not work after a couple of times, do not keep trying; other occasions will present themselves.*
● *Confront one and only one issue at a time. Do not be tempted to bring up other issues that are bothering you when you feel the person is open to discussion and willing to listen.*

As well as the various skills you will need in order to deal with difficult people, you should also learn some strategies to deal with the more common types of difficult behaviour. Some of these occur over and over again, and the more proficient you are at dealing with them the more successful you will be at managing the people exhibiting that behaviour.

Some of the most common forms of difficult behaviour include manipulative or avoidant behaviour, put-downs and humiliation, and direct aggression. There is a different set of steps to follow when dealing with each of these.

★REMEMBER!

Dealing with difficult people or behaviour can:
- *Lower your self-esteem by undermining your value and competence. It can sow seeds of self-doubt and lower your self-confidence.*

- *Trigger unhelpful or defensive behaviour patterns, for example direct or indirect aggression.*
- *Stimulate debilitating feelings of distress, helplessness, embarrassment or anger.*

PUT-DOWNS AND DEROGATORY REMARKS

Most people are familiar with finding themselves on the receiving end of remarks that are intended to humiliate, or statements that have an underlying sexist or racist intent. Often the put-down or sexist response may be nonverbal rather than verbal, for example, the adoption of a patronizing tone of voice with emphasis on certain words, or an upward raising of the eyes.

Put-downs and derogatory remarks are difficult to respond to because of the indirect or unstated message. If you pick the person up on it at the time you may end up looking more neurotic or feeling worse than if you had let it go. You fear that you may have

misinterpreted what they were really saying or that you overreacted to the situation.

This confusion arises partly because put-downs and criticism from others hurts most when they touch on areas of your vulnerability. If you were feeling good about yourself the comment would not be so paralysing.

Dealing with put-downs
If the derogatory comment or put-down is direct, your first step in dealing with it is self-disclosure. Tell the other person how you are feeling, for example 'I feel hurt by your comment. What do you mean?'

The next step is called repetition and fielding. You may get a response from the

person that he was 'only joking'. In this case you acknowledge their position (called fielding) and repeat your feeling. 'To you it may be a joke but I feel . . .'

If the put-down is indirect and ambiguous, as in 'We don't seem to be getting far, do we?' (which implies that it is your fault), and you think the comment is not just sheer nastiness, then negative inquiry can be useful. You might say 'Are you suggesting that I am inadequate as a manager?' This technique will either draw the genuine criticism or expose the nastiness, making it easier to respond.

Often put-downs and derogatory comments are not dealt with at the

time, either because you are paralysed with emotions such as fear, embarrassment or anger, or because other issues are more important. In these cases the full expression of the feeling, or full acknowledgement of the depth of feeling to yourself, relieves the tension sufficiently to mount a challenge and/or to affirm your dignity and value.

Remember, it is never too late to pick up the statement and deal with the person concerned. Do not forget your request/demand about how you want the person to behave in the future. People tend to forget this, and wonder why the same situations recur.

MANIPULATIVE OR AVOIDANT BEHAVIOUR

When dealing with people who avoid issues or try and manipulate, you should:

● First make a request. 'I would like you to produce your work by next week as you agreed.' The reply might be 'Well, my typewriter has broken down and I have taken it to be mended. I'm not sure when I'll have it back.'

● You should then acknowledge the difficulty of the person and repeat your request. 'I appreciate it may be difficult for you without your typewriter but I would still like you to produce the work on time.'

● This simple assertive technique is called 'Broken Record' and consists of repeating your request while, at the same time, empathizing with the position of the

avoider or manipulator.

● Do not fall into the trap of uncovering the avoidant or manipulative behaviour unless you particularly want to.

● Be persistent; the

technique is surprisingly effective. It may need to be enhanced by negotiating a workable compromise if the person adopts a levelling or assertive way of interacting.

PERSONAL ATTACKS AND DIRECT AGGRESSION

You have probably experienced personal attacks at one time or another. These may take the form of personal abuse, including blaming and threatening behaviour. They are similar to put-downs but are usually more direct and aggressive.

One method of dealing with such attacks stresses the need to diffuse the aggression and move the interaction from the aggressive to an assertive mode as quickly as possible.

● When you are first faced with such an attack you should stop. Play for time, and do not react in kind.

● Next, request clarification and check for understanding. Ask the person 'Do you mean . . .? How do you see it . . .? Tell me more.' Being listened to usually disarms and defuses the aggression. It also gives you time to think and provides you with more specific information about the problem.

● Make a statement of your beliefs and opinions. These may be preceded by an acknowledgement of the feelings, or the perspective, of the aggressor. 'I appreciate how you feel but this is my opinion.'

● Should the aggression continue you can do one of two things. You can state your position more strongly, or you can draw attention to any discrepancy between your present and former behaviour, or between the person's present or former view of you.

For example, 'I don't think I am stupid. I would like to point out that you yourself praised my work on our previous projects.'

● Should the aggression continue, you can make clear to the person how their behaviour is affecting you, and

what the consequences of their continuing the behaviour will be. For example, 'When you keep shouting at me like that I feel angry. If you continue I shall have no option but to call in our boss, though I would prefer not to.' If you have no sanctions, or choose not to use them, the second part of this intervention is not a good idea. In any case, it must only be used as a last resort.

If none of these works you can end the interaction, or get the other person to talk about the strong feelings behind the attack.

Everybody, whether they acknowledge it or not, needs support in some form or another, both from other people and themselves. Support can range from simple greeting or welcoming, through praise and appreciation to giant acts of benevolence and constructive patronage. You can be supported as a person through having your values, way of being and who you are affirmed, or by an advocate who stands up for your rights and needs.

Your beliefs, norms, values and morals can be supported, and so can your actions and creations. Most fundamentally, you are supported by being loved, that is, by somebody taking delight in and facilitating both your growth and the development of your personal potential.

YOUR SUPPORT SYSTEM MAP

To explore the supportive quality of your relationships, you can draw them out in a map. Take a large piece of paper, put yourself in the middle, then map out all the other people, groups, places, animals, objects and activities which you experience as supportive.

You may like to draw a picture of each of these, putting the important ones closer to you, and the less important farther away. Put in arrows to show the direction of support – is the support mutual or one way?

Your map may include a number of people, such as peers, subordinates, spouses, children, parents, relatives, current and old friends, neighbours and professional, religious or spiritual teachers. Allow yourself to include your whole world in its widest sense.

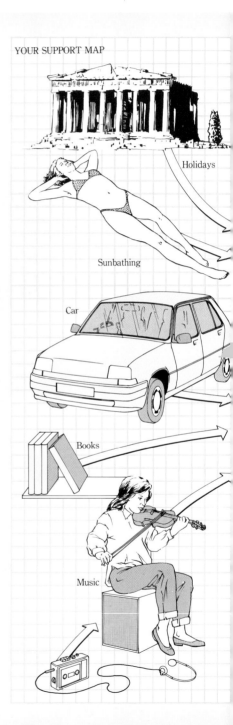

YOUR SUPPORT MAP

Holidays

Sunbathing

Car

Books

Music

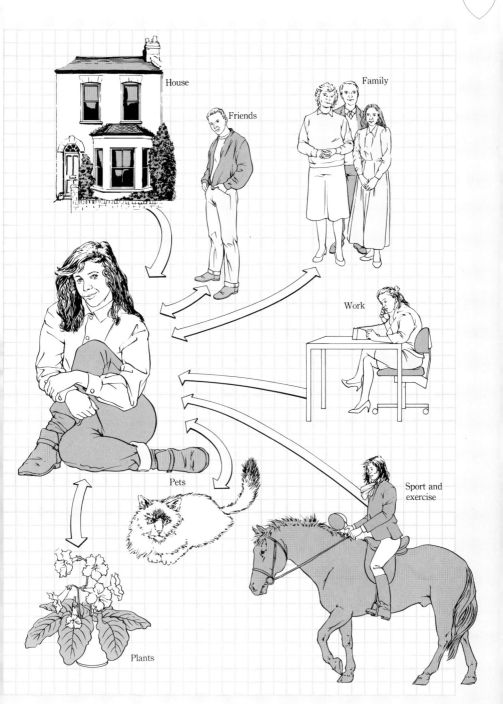

House

Friends

Family

Work

Pets

Sport and exercise

Plants

There are a number of questions you should explore with regard to your attitudes toward support systems. These include determining where, with whom and how you support your life and work. Do you use your support system effectively? Do you even believe in getting support?

Developing and learning to use support systems acknowledges that everyone as an individual can take responsibility for themselves, and in doing so can be aware of their need for support. And, at its best, the notion of support encompasses both encouragement and challenge.

DETERMINE YOUR ATTITUDE

The idea of support is contradictory in our society. Some people feel that support enables them to cope by ensuring that they do not have to go it alone, while others have the idea that to admit that they need help is a sign of weakness.

To explore your attitudes, try the following word association exercise. You can either do this on your own, or with a friend or colleague.

What words do you associate with support? List them, allowing your mind to wander around these words, free associating from one to the other. This will allow your unconscious mind as well as your conscious to begin to get a feel for the range of attitudes and images that you

connect with the word.

When you have done this, look at your list and ring those words that have a positive and encouraging tone to them. Then underline those with a negative and discouraging tone.

Pick a couple of positive words and a couple of negative ones that seem important to you. Continue the free association further. For example, if a negative word is 'props', list all the associations with it – such as weak, not strong enough or fragile. If a positive word is 'foundation', list associations such as strong, able to take the strain, base, essential or vital.

As you do this pay attention to your feelings and to the images and memories

you become aware of. These may be personal stories and messages about the idea of support, stories of your childhood and the lessons you were taught about receiving support. Allow yourself to remember all these lessons; they are all part of the way in which you constructed your current attitude to support.

You may find there is a 'pivot point' between your attitudes. On the one side you value support and see it as enabling, while on the other you devalue support and see it as smothering or limiting. The devaluing attitudes need voicing and acknowledging. If you do not admit to them they may be heard indirectly and

be destructive to any attempts you may make to value support.

Once you have determined your attitudes about support, go back to your support map and look at it again. If your attitude is that only weak people need support, you may realize that your support system is very meagre; if your attitude is that you cannot do anything on your own, you may find you have so much support it prevents you doing anything for yourself.

If you are uncertain about how supportive your relationships are, you may find it helpful to draw an 'anti-support' map, which would highlight those ones that sap your strength, undermine and sabotage you.

★ TRY THIS NOW!

To review your current needs, make a list of all the ways in which you would really like support. Alongside this list, write down all the different ways of getting it.

What are the things you do that stop you from getting support? Finally, list some simple things you could do to get more support where you need it.

★ REMEMBER!

When you are asking for support, you need to beware of that which, although well intentioned, may turn out to be smothering, rescuing or unhelpful, or deprives you of

opportunities to realize your potential.

The key question to ask in this situation is: 'Whose needs are being met?'

YOUR NEGATIVE SUPPORT MAP

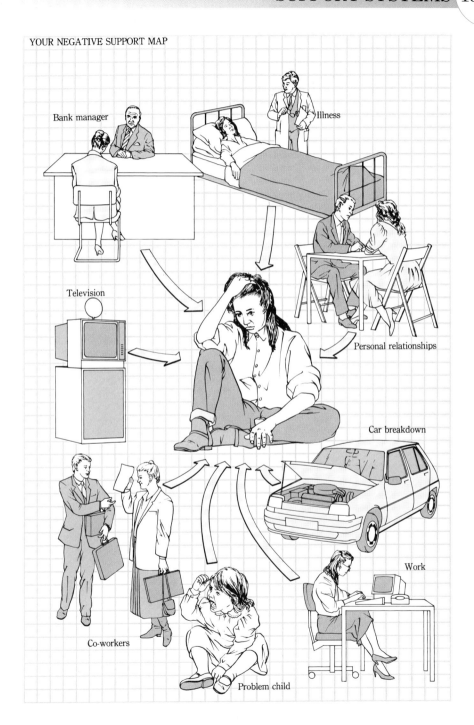

Bank manager

Illness

Television

Personal relationships

Car breakdown

Work

Co-workers

Problem child

Sharing is a support, and a supportive relationship with one other person with whom you share your current trials and joys can be a great resource. This important other person may be your partner, a loyal friend from school days, or a colleague with whom you have mutual trust and respect.

We all need different people to help us meet different needs, and it is unrealistic to expect one person to meet all your needs. The challenge is to maintain and nurture these important relationships so that they are mutually rewarding rather than manipulative or abusive.

ANALYSE HELPFUL RELATIONSHIPS

Current relationships

From your support map, identify an important relationship. Who is this person for you? Make a list of their qualities.

Take some crayons and draw a picture of the other person. See what colours and shapes you choose to represent them. Ask yourself these questions:
● Who do they remind you of?
● What would happen if they disappeared?
● What would you miss and what would you gain?
● In what ways is this relationship supportive to you?
● In what ways is it not supportive?

Types of support

Basically, there are three different kinds of support.
● Nurturing support is that which prepares you to do things. It is gentle and accepting.
● Energizing support is more confronting and challenging. It helps to bring out the lively and creative side of you.
● Relaxing support helps you tidy up and finish things off. It also gets you away from work so that you can relax and recharge your inner batteries.

In looking at your current relationships, what kind of support do you get from them? Make a list of how the relationship gives you support in each of these three categories.

Working together

While it is helpful to conduct these exercises on your own at first, it will help you develop the supportive qualities of a relationship if you also do them with the other person. Any of the above exercises can be shared, and following are more exercises you can do together as ways of exploring, maintaining and nurturing your relationship.

Sit opposite each other and take it in turns to give answers to the question 'Who are you for me?' After a while move on to the questions 'What do you give me, and what do I give you?' After doing this pause and reflect on how you are both feeling and whether you are satisfied.

Finally, make three specific requests of each other, and discuss which you feel you can meet.

UNHELPFUL RELATIONSHIPS

Occasionally, when you take time to evaluate a relationship, you may find that it is more draining than supportive and so have to face up to ending or changing it.

One way of saying goodbye is to voice your resentments, say what you have appreciated about the relationship, and acknowledge that it is now over.

There are certain unhelpful relationships which, by their very nature, cannot be ended. You may have a boss that you find unsupportive, or work with another employee of the company who is unsupportive and draining.

It is useful to acknowledge to yourself the limitations and drains of the relationship. This first step will enable you to find ways of limiting the damage they cause and help you find other sources of the support you need.

NEW RELATIONSHIPS

You may decide that you need to establish a new support relationship. The following strategies may be helpful to ensure you develop the type of relationship you want and require.

● Be clear about what you want from the relationship. Make a list of what you are looking for and what you do not need.

● Think about who might meet these needs. A current acquaintance might be able to help, but also be prepared to seek out the right person. Go for the best in getting what you want.

● Arrange a meeting to discuss what you want. Be prepared to say exactly what you are looking for.

● Be prepared to acknowledge and say clearly if it appears that the relationship will not offer what you need.

● Find out what the other person wants and how the relationship meets their needs.

● Both of you must be aware of the extent of your commitment. Determine when, how often and where you will meet, what sort of relationship it will be, and whether it is a mutually supportive relationship or one way. Any payment or other exchanges should be very clearly agreed.

YOUR LIST

What I am looking for

What I do not need

Groups form for several purposes. Some, such as management teams, are there to do a task. Others, such as social clubs and athletic teams, are there to help members do things they want. Support groups as such are set up solely to give emotional or practical support to some kind of personal or professional activity.

Of course, groups can be both support groups and task groups; indeed, the best task groups are, by their very nature, supportive. A management team will have a task and will also be aware that if it is to work well time must be taken to review the task and to build and maintain the relationships within the team. For any group to be supportive, a basic and primary question you must ask is 'For what aspects of my life and work do I want this group to support me, and how?'

SETTING UP A SUPPORT GROUP

If there is no existing group for the type of support you need, you may need to consider setting one up. This can easily be done.

It may be with people with whom you work, or share a common interest. If, for example, you want support as a woman in a management position, you may choose to get this from a group of women who are also your peers, a group of women from all walks of life, or from your immediate colleagues, both men and women.

When you are establishing the group:
● Be clear about what you want from the group.
● Go for what you want first, and only compromise if it becomes difficult or problematic.
● Contact the people with whom you would like to form the group, and be clear about your needs and the commitment you are thinking of in terms of time, money and availability.
● Agree to get together for an initial meeting to establish that needs can be met in a reciprocal way.
● Agree to meet a specified number of times, and then to review how helpful the group is and whether (and how) it should continue.
● Agree when the group will be open to new members. If membership is steady this will help to build trust.

Informal support group

SUPPORT GROUP GUIDELINES

Once the group is established there are a number of guidelines you can follow to help it function successfully.
- Go gently to begin with to help build up trust.
- Give each member equal time to say how they are and what they need.
- Treat each member with fundamental respect.
- Listen to each other, and do not steal each other's time with your own stories.

- Draw up an agenda based on members' needs and allocate time to each item. If you need more time than expected for an item, renegotiate the agenda. Do not just let things drag on.
- Respect the confidentiality of the group; do not gossip about other members.
- Acknowledge what has been achieved and note any unfinished business.
- Periodically review whether the group is meeting the needs of the members.

PROVIDING FEEDBACK

The group should provide supportive challenges by members' giving each other positive and negative feedback. One way of doing this is through self- and peer-assessment. The group as a whole needs to agree to use this procedure, and to decide on a time structure which is fair to all members.
- First, each member takes time on their own to review themselves and their performance and to identify the strengths and weaknesses which are important to them. The group may or may not have agreed common criteria for doing this beforehand.

- Next, each member presents their self-assessment to the group.
- The group then gives feedback. First, it should be confronting feedback pointing to aspects of performance the person has overlooked, or where their self-assessment appears to be in error. Second is supportive and affirming feedback concerning the person's strengths and capabilities, either unmentioned in the assessment or overlooked.
- Finally, each individual reviews their performance in the light of the assessment, making plans for future work.

Formal support group

Giving yourself support is important. It lets you take responsibility for your own health and well-being, and allows you to use the support of others effectively. Self-support comes primarily from liking and loving yourself, valuing the wisdom of your mind, body and spirit.

People spend a lot of time criticizing themselves and putting themselves down. Truly to develop the ability to support yourself you need to identify and be able to love yourself unconditionally. If you can do this you will have developed an invaluable resource.

MANAGING TIME

One of the ways in which you can give yourself support is to use your time effectively. To do this, you should review the way you use time. Examine the way you spend each day, week, month, and year. Look also at the rhythm and pattern of your life.
● Make a list of the things that you do that are self-supporting.
● Identify the time in each week/month which you currently devote to them. Is it enough? If not, what do you need to do to make more time?
● Then list all the things you do which sabotage your plans and which keep you from doing these self-supportive things.
● Write down how you could use your support network to help you stop sabotaging yourself and be true to your self-knowledge.

YOUR SELF-SUPPORT LIST

Methods of self-support	Time given	What gets in way	Use of network

ECOLOGICAL SUPPORT

You are supported by your environment – your home and office, the country you live in and the earth you dwell on. All are part of a huge support system which needs you as much as you need it.

It is this mutual support system that you can most take for granted and be most distant from. You need to alert your mind and consciousness to the global system of which you are a part – the universal self-support system – in order for the system to work well.

That is a lot to take in, so start small by considering your immediate environment, and work outward from there. How could you change your home or workplace, even in a small way, so that it is more supportive? You might like a new chair or fresh flowers on your desk. Or you could appreciate better ventilation or more natural light.

Going further afield, remember the places that were included on your support map. Imagine each place vividly, and identify the qualities that are important to you. Try consciously to visit them regularly. If walking on a sunny morning refreshes you, make sure you walk rather than drive or take public transportation. What ways do you have in your power to preserve and maintain these supports?

Further afield still, consider the support that you receive from the planet and the natural resources of clean air, water and sunshine. Just as we need to take care of our immediate environment, our home and workplace, so also we live in a mutual relationship with our planet.

As with all mutual support systems, time spent caring for the environment will be repaid. So, by doing something locally, find some way of giving support and caring for the environment.

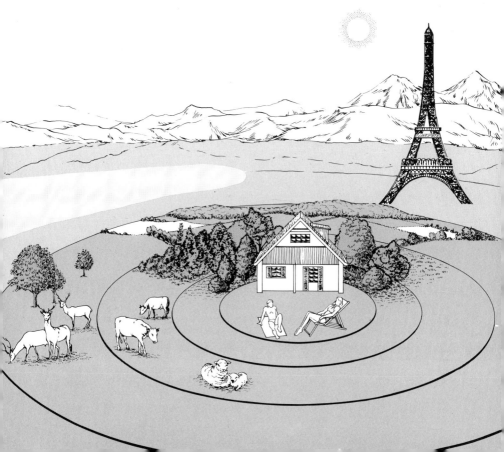

Life is rarely placid. Instead, it has a number of ups and downs which you can accept if you do not become stuck in one place for too long. Movement, change and development seem to be what most people flourish on and learn from.

If you acknowledge and accept these ups and downs you keep moving. It is more difficult to move on and learn if you get stuck over worrying about the lows, blaming yourself and other people. Or, if you try to hold on to the highs and do not acknowledge that they too must pass, you may find yourself in a situation of false reality and fail to see what remains to be done in your life.

THE RHYTHM OF LIFE

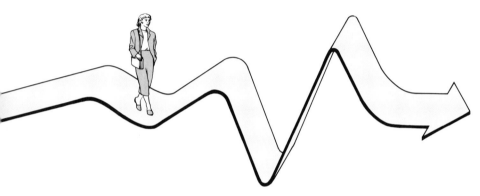

Traditionally, the seasons of the year are marked by rituals. The coming of spring, the flowering of summer, the abundance of harvest, and the depths of winter are all marked by religious and secular festivals.

These rituals are ways of acknowledging the rhythm of life, ways of seeing that things pass with the seasons. Most people have smaller rituals which mark the passing of each day and each week – the early morning cup of tea or the arrival of the newspaper.

You should recognize and acknowledge the high and low points, the more minor ups and downs of your daily life. Find a way of giving them their due. It then becomes easier to move on to the next part of your life. This means finding little rituals which take care of these times in ways that enable you to then let them go. Some possible ways of doing this are:

● In a peer group or family situation, agree on a time when everyone has a chance to share resentments about the trivial things that have not gone well. Similarly, it can be useful to allow time for everyone to say what has gone well, what they have achieved and what is going well for them at the moment.

● At the end of a difficult day, have a shower and imagine that the water is washing away your cares and worries. Changing your clothes with awareness and intent can help you leave one role of yourself behind and free you to adopt another.

● Identify the objects or small tasks which support your ability to move from lows to highs. For example, buying some flowers, making a telephone call, having a shower, putting your feet up.

SUPPORT FOR A CRISIS

As well as the more minor ups and downs, life has its major crises and emergencies. By the very nature of an emergency there is little forward planning you can do. But you can learn from the past.

There are usually four stages in a person's response to a major crisis. The first of these is shock, which means that the person needs taking care of. This is followed by denial or rejection of the situation, and then by a more or less gradual recognition and acceptance of the new state of affairs.

Finally, the crisis is integrated into normal life, and the lessons are learned. A crisis will be unfinished if any stage is unresolved.

Remember a crisis or emergency from either your home or work life. Write down the experience, or tell it to a friend. Draw some simple sketches that remind you of what happened. Then reflect on your response. Can you identify the four stages outlined above? Are there any that remain unresolved? What is needed to integrate and complete it?

STAGES OF RESPONSE TO CRISIS

Shock

Denial or rejection

Acceptance

Integration

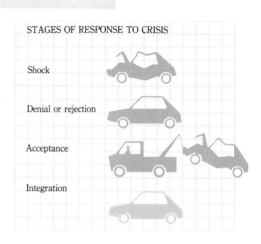

SUPPORT FOR TRANSITIONS

Our society is changing, and the major transitions in life are now less clear than they once were. Do we come of age at 16, 18, or 21? Retire at 55, 60 or 80? People may change career many times in their lives, and in more egalitarian workplaces promotion is less visible than in the past.

In times of transition there is a lot of confusion, which is both bewildering and exciting. The emotions you may have at these times need recognizing. You need the support of friends and relatives, and can be helped by having clear markers or gateways from one stage of your life to the next.

At the next important transition in your life – be it your birthday, or a new contract, or the end of an important project of work – invent for yourself a small ceremony that marks the change. This could be very simple.

For example, at the completion of a report have it nicely bound and show it to your colleagues. Or at the beginning of a new project support yourself by getting together exactly the right equipment for the job or by redesigning your workplace. Do this with an intent that marks the transition, as well as simply addressing the task.

SUPPORT FOR SUCCESS

When something goes well, or a task is finished, it is natural to celebrate in some way. But the smaller, day to day achievements tend to get overlooked. They, too, need recognizing, with simple, small and specific acknowledgments which give positive feedback and support.

Society often tells us not to boast, which may lead you to ignore what is going well for you. You should find ways to celebrate the achievements of your life. This includes the little ones as well as the big ones, the everyday delights as well as the resounding triumphs.

It may be that you reward yourself when a project has gone well, or that you invite friends to dinner to share your good news. Times of success are also times for support, and you will probably find it helpful to look for ways of involving others in your celebrations.

The first group to which you belonged was probably your family. As with all first experiences, your experience in your family instilled in you a set of beliefs about how people should and do interact in groups.

This experience also helped you acquire skills or strategies with which to survive and influence groups. You bring these expectations, skills and beliefs to the various groups you join later in life.

EXPECTATIONS OF GROUPS

Because your own family is unique to you, your ideas of how people interact, your expectations and skills are different from those of other people. When members of different families come together with internalized rules and expectations, the interactions can become complex.

Many people tend to fall back on the ways of relating that worked in their family. More often than not these ways of relating are not flexible enough to see you through the different kinds of groups you later join.

It is important to get to know as much as you can about the expectations and preferred roles which you acquired in your own family so that you can choose the most appropriate way of behaving in other group situations and, if necessary, develop new skills.

TYPES OF GROUPS

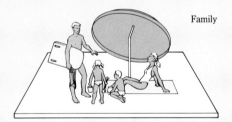

Family

Board of directors

Athletic team

Therapy group

There are many types of groups, most of which work in different ways and require specific knowledge and participation skills. Natural groups like the family may have a number of purposes, but created groups such as committees, teams or therapy groups will often have only a single purpose.

Clearly families and committees, for example, work very differently. So it is important to get to know how different types of group function if you are to participate in them effectively.

However, while there are very obvious differences between groups, there also seems to be a great similarity in the way diverse groups function. This is mainly because people who comprise these groups are similar and have set ways of behaving.

The way people interact in groups is called group dynamics. By learning about general group dynamics you can enhance the way you function in groups.

RISKS AND BENEFITS OF GROUPS

HEALTHY GROUP FUNCTIONING

There are both risks and benefits attached to participating in groups and being a group member. You can develop a range of skills which apply information about group dynamics. You can then use these skills in ways that maximize these benefits and minimize the risks.

The benefits
Compared with the individual, the group is more robust. It can survive and continue to perform even when one individual leaves it. Other benefits include:
● Producing higher quality results.
● Making more efficient use of resources.
● Minimizing responsibility of any one member for the outcome of the task.
● Increased levels of commitment.
● The ability to make more risky decisions.
● Reducing possible error by combining judgement.
● Producing solutions that are more creative.
● Easing the sense of isolation of individual members and meeting their needs for belonging.

The risks
Not all group participation is beneficial. There are risks involved, and you need to be aware that groups can also have inhibiting or destructive potential. You will probably recognize some of the following risks from your own personal experience.
● Making an individual the scapegoat, or becoming the scapegoat yourself, for the group.
● Unnecessary conformist or compliant behaviour.
● Apathy, boredom and withdrawal from active participation.
● Personality clashes and destructive, competitive or conflict behaviour.
● Group functioning at the lowest common denominator.
● Inappropriate dominance by some members.
  Of course, these risks and benefits will occur to a greater or lesser degree depending on a variety of factors. These include the size and location of the group, tasks and decision-making procedures.

For a group to function in a healthy manner, there are a number of pointers that can be followed. A group needs:
● A common purpose, or something that helps the group to be homogenous and cohesive.
● A means of organization that enables members to achieve their common purpose, for example appointment of a chairman, treasurer or secretary.
● Common recognition by members of group boundaries, that is, who belongs, who does not, and how membership is decided.
● A capacity to

absorb and lose members without losing group identity.
● The ability to adapt and grow, that is, to go through various group development and performance cycles while maintaining its integrity and direction.
● To be free from exclusive and inhibiting internal subgroupings, for example, the formation of cliques.
● Individuals who are valued for their contributions to the group and are free to act within generally accepted group norms or rules.
● A capacity to face discontent and resolve conflict between members.

★ TRY THIS NOW!

Make a list of the groups in which you participate.
● *What do you like/ dislike in each?*
● *What purposes/ needs do they fulfil?*

● *Do they function well/badly? In what ways?*
● *How could you improve their functioning?*

One way of getting to know yourself is by looking at the way you handle the process of joining and participating in a group. Group members must come to terms with three important factors as defined by William Shutz, an expert on encounter groups – inclusion, control and affection.

What do I want and
do I want to be here?

Does the leader include/exclude me?

Do other people include/exclude me?

INCLUSION

When you join a group you will have some idea of what the group aims to do. This motivates you to come along in the first place. Once you are there a subtle process of checking out takes place. You may ask yourself questions such as:
● What do I want and do I want to be here?
● Does the leader include/exclude me?

● Do other participants include/exclude me?
These issues are checked out each time you join a new group.
Other factors which affect the outcome of this checking out are:
● Your ability to include yourself and others, for example by engaging in social talk, welcoming and greeting and self-

disclosure.
● Your interest in becoming part of this group. Besides the official aim of the group people often have other desires, some of which they are open about, but others that are more private. Some desires may be unconscious and are often called the 'hidden agenda'. The more unrelated these aims are from the official aim the

less likely they are to be met.
● Similarity between yourself and other group members. These similarities include social status, culture and educational achievements. Feeling out of place does not auger well for developing a sense of belonging and being accepted as a group member, which is at the nub of inclusion.

CONTROL

Influence is central to control. How and whether influence is used to meet your needs are crucial. People in a group will have differing needs and aims, even where there is agreement on the official aim. Some needs will probably be met, others not

even expressed.
You will find that if you ask yourself the following questions a general pattern of answers will emerge:
● Do I want to and do I dare try to influence the group?
● Does the leader respond to my efforts to meet my needs?

● Do participants block or support my efforts to influence?
● Will I still be included if I am successful, or even if I am not?
Some people, from their past experience, resort to domineering or manipulative means of getting their needs met.

In the short term, the manipulative approach may be effective, but in the longer term levelling or assertive approaches are likely to cause less resentment and be less likely to result in passive or active exclusion from group activity.

★ TRY THIS NOW!

- Imagine that a film maker could create some images of your interaction with your family and friends as a six-year-old.
- What roles did you play? Who were the significant figures (present or absent, real or fantasy) in your life at that time? How did you relate to them?
- Now imagine an interested Martian is trying to figure out what roles you play presently and how you interact. What would he observe watching you participate in groups today? List his observations.
- Do you notice any similarities or carry over between the two sets of observations? What do they tell you about your interaction patterns? Are there any new roles you might try? What do you imagine would happen if you did? Are your current patterns helpful or inhibiting?

AFFECTION

Perhaps the most important question you will ask when being a group member is whether the other members like or love you.

What is being checked out here is spontaneous expressions of love and affection. These may be expressions of care or appreciation, or they may be supportive touch or acts of giving which imply affection.

People who are relating at this level do not always have to be asked for support but delight in the growth, the vitality and the performance of others. Questions you might ask yourself include:
- Will I show affection, and will I accept loving?
- Does the leader like me?
- Do participants show affection for me or have I got genuine friends in the group?

ADDRESSING THE ISSUES

Each of the three issues, inclusion, control and affection, need to be addressed by each individual in any group, and in that order. So each person usually needs to be able to include or exclude themselves before they can effectively influence or control. Failure to manage the control issue may make it impossible to meet your needs.

Assuming you develop the ability to influence the group, and your needs can be met in an acceptable way, you will usually begin dealing with the affection issue.

Once you are sure of being liked and of liking, you may feel free to take risks which are on the borders of acceptability in the group. As a result you will move through the three stages again and again, each time increasing the sense of belonging.

Static groups, in which people are not taking risks and are not moving through these cycles, are usually mediocre in terms of the return they give to participants on an emotional level. Low motivation and commitment are often reflected in these types of group.

ROLES

Another way of getting to know about the way you function in groups is to spend some time looking at the type of roles which you choose or tend to get stuck with. How you understand groups, what you expect to happen in groups, and the roles you tend to adopt are usually learned in your family and re-enacted in present day groups.

Identifying the roles you held in your family, and relating them to your present way of participating in a group, can give insight into your behaviour. It can enable you to be more flexible in the roles you adopt.

★ TEST YOURSELF!

Think of a group in which you are currently a participant. With regard to inclusion, control and affection, how are you managing each of these issues in the group so far?

Which one is important to you at the moment? Is there any way you can improve the way in which you deal with these issues?

A useful distinction can be made between what a group does, that is, its task, goals and aims, and how the group does it, for example the process or method it uses. Often people concentrate on the task and pay little attention to the process or the dynamics of the group.

Knowing what to look for is essential if you are to participate more effectively in any group and change what is going wrong.

WHAT TO LOOK FOR

It is important to be clear about the group's purpose to avoid unnecessary frustration and conflict. This will help you determine whether the group will be able to meet your private personal goals as well as the group's official ones.

Goals and aims
Your private goals and aims of a group may complicate matters. Sometimes, even the declared purpose of a group may not be its real purpose. For example, a committee, which is ostensibly there to take decisions, may be used to rubber stamp decisions taken prior to the meeting.

Participation
Patterns of group participation can be informative once they are interpreted and checked out.
● Who are the high/low contributors?
● Who are the silent people in the group. How is their silence interpreted? Is it consent, dissent or fear?
● Who talks/does not talk to whom? Who interrupts or follows whom in conversation? Is there any reason why this should be so?

Influence and leadership
There are different kinds of leader in a group. It may be that there is one official leader, or there may be many. There can also be unofficial leaders.
● The responsible leader is the accountable person.
● The effective leader is the person whose proposals or suggestions are most likely to be taken up.
● The psychological leader is the one who group members are most likely to identify with emotionally.
Sometimes all three of these positions can be invested in the same person, but more often they are occupied by three different people. You may find in your groups that it is useful to rotate or delegate the leadership and other roles to prevent the group from stagnating.
Sometimes conflict occurs between the responsible leader and the effective leader, and at times the effective leader and the psychological leader pull against one another. Cooperation between these three leaders is essential if the group is to function well.

The style of influence or leadership is crucial. Different groups require different styles of leadership. For example, a committee requires a more democratic style in its leader than a yacht crew.

Group roles
Any group organizes itself in order to achieve its goals. The roles people take are important to group dynamics.
Besides roles such as secretary, chairman or captain,

you might have a role such as rebel, scapegoat, bully, timekeeper or critic. While some roles might seem to be unhelpful, there is often an aspect of the role which is important to the group. For example the clown, despite his disciplinary laxities, helps a group to relax and have a laugh.
Apart from the leader, ask yourself who takes what roles in your groups. Are these roles inhibiting or beneficial?

Making decisions

Decisions can be made by majority vote, by consensus or by unanimous decision only. Each style of decision making will have consequences for the morale of the group and the follow-up action related to the decisions. In your groups:

● Do some people impose autocratic decisions on others?
● Is there any proposing, consulting and supporting?
● Is there any negotiating, bargaining or compromising?
● Are some people's proposals always adopted or other's always ignored?
● Do some people abstain from decision making?
    What is the effect of these behaviours on the group? Are there any reasons why they continue to occur? What would need to happen for a change to take place?

Group atmosphere

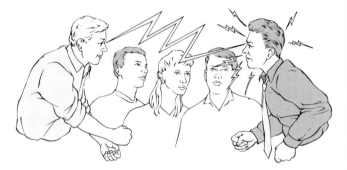

What is the atmosphere, climate and morale of the group? Is it friendly and congenial, or tense and sluggish? Often it is difficult to put your finger on why the group is the way it is. The cause is usually buried in the group's past. But how a group maintains its atmosphere is easier to identify.

● Do group members attack or withdraw rather than relate constructively?
● Are they dependent on one or a few members, for example, to achieve the task or nurture one another?
● Do people pair off or develop cliques or subgroups which destroy the unity of the group?
● Is there any sense of collective achievement or fun?

● Do people harmonize in nurturing, preparing, performing, and relaxing, or are people all over the place and uncoordinated?
    These are common areas of malfunctions in groups and often reflect poor leadership. Failure to attend to the tasks in hand or routine maintenance of a group may render it ineffective.

★ TRY THIS NOW!

Identify the norms of a group in which you participate and separate those with positive and negative outcomes for the group.
    Share these with a colleague from the group and check them out. Ask the group if they are interested in your findings.

★ TEST YOURSELF!

Choose one or two groups in which you participate and use each heading to examine what these groups are like.
● *Is this knowledge useful? How?*
● *Could you make some suggestions based on this information which would raise your level of satisfaction, and the level of others in the group?*

Norms and ground rules

The behaviours that are or are not acceptable in a group are defined by norms and ground rules. These may be implicit or explicit and may help or hinder group functioning. Norms will be different for each group and there will not necessarily be agreement among members as to what norms are operating.
    Following are some examples, both helpful and inhibiting, of norms found in groups.

● One person talks at a time.
● It is acceptable for some members to be late but not others.
● Feelings are not talked about or expressed.
● Sex is not discussed.
● Conflict between members is avoided.
● Decisions are only made by the leader.
● Too much initiative is resented.

Each person who comes to the group brings a set of needs, expectations, resources, skills, and previous group experience. Group dynamics, which are interactions between members, are intricate and subtle and can be difficult to track.

If you try to reduce their complexity you run the risk of misinterpreting the facts. On the other hand, if you do not have some way of categorizing the complexity of the way in which the group functions you will be overcome by confusion.

MAPPING A GROUP

The following is one way of mapping or tracking group dynamics, developed by social scientists. It outlines the five stages of development in the life of a group, which are forming, storming, norming, performing and mourning.

Once you know about group dynamics this knowledge should help you be a little less anxious about the early stages of group development which can, of necessity, be a little difficult.

These stages will also enable you to guide the group toward a more effective functioning by engaging in each stage as fully as possible. However, never mistake ways of mapping group dynamics for the reality. They are but pale reflections of it, although they can help predict or categorize what goes on in groups.

Forming
This stage is usually characterized by greetings and welcomes. People are usually checking out whether they feel they can belong to or be included in the group, what roles they might take, and what they are supposed to be doing.

During the forming stage people often share a little about theselves and ask questions of others. This is the time to find out what the limits and boundaries, the purpose and nature of the group is. This is when they check expectations and generally settle in.

Storming
This stage involves competition for position. It can be overt or covert and can be difficult to recognize.

During storming people may attack, withdraw or assert themselves. They may try to set up cliques or absent themselves physically or emotionally. Or they may try to dominate in their efforts to ensure that their needs are met.

This phase might also be described as one of rebellion – against the leader, the ground rules or

how things are done. It is a time of testing the limits and exploring what is possible, and is usually an uncomfortable phase for the group.

However, it is necessary to see storming through, otherwise the rebelliousness keeps emerging in various unhelpful forms, most notably in lack of cohesion or togetherness later in the life of the group. This is the crucial sorting out process in which members come to terms with each other.

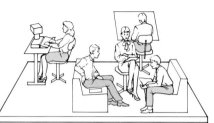

Norming

The initial stages are those during which people have tested each other and the leader out, and the group has been able to contain any conflict and work it through. The group can then usually agree on ways of functioning (norms) which will guide their collective behaviour toward effective performance. At this stage people begin to take responsibility for roles rather than deny responsibility as they once did.

These norms may be helpful or unhelpful. They sometimes need to be made explicit by asking questions such as 'What can I do and what can I not do in this group?'

Performing

At this stage group members are cooperating with one another to achieve the goals of the group and meet each other's needs.

Groups functioning well at this stage often harmonize around nurturing, energizing, performing and relaxing. Members:
● Care, help and inform each other (nurturing).
● Plan, imagine and challenge (energizing).
● Carry out plans and implement solutions (performing).
● Celebrate, reflect or review (relaxing).

In this way both the task and the emotional needs of the group are fulfilled.

Mourning

This stage of the group is the end phase. It is often characterized by a loosening of the bonds between people and a fall off in attempts to influence the group. During mourning there is an increasing tendency for group members to exclude themselves from the business of the group.

In short, a reversal occurs of the inclusion, control and affection cycle. Often there is a reluctance to come to terms with the fact that the group is ending. Many do not want to face the personal loss or perhaps face the fact that membership of the group may not have been very satisfactory.

Group members may feel that much unfinished business still exists, either of a task or an interpersonal nature. It is important for members to persevere and clear up any unfinished business and be able to celebrate before leaving.

★ TEST YOURSELF!

● *Does the concept of stages help illuminate the dynamics of any groups to which you belong?*
● *What stage are they functioning at now?*
● *What does the group need next in order to progress?*
● *Have previous stages been entered into and worked through? If not, what signs suggest this and what needs to happen?*

When you are participating in a group, there are a number of different tasks you might have as a member. These tasks will usually change depending on the stage of development the group is in (see pp. 152–153).

It is important for you to accomplish these goals or tasks if you are to become an active member, help the group in its goals and accomplish and obtain what you need from the group itself.

YOUR TASKS AS A GROUP MEMBER

In the first stage of group development your main tasks are to clarify what you want, what the group is trying to do, and how you as an individual fit into the group. In the second, or storming, stage the individual's task is to survive and engage in the challenging, the bids for power and the various struggles which are necessary to establish a healthy, functioning group.

In the norming phase the individual needs to contribute to the formation of constructive group rules, which will ensure an effective and efficient working relationship between members. Full engagement in the creation of these norms, responsibility for them and commitment to them is needed from all participants.

In the performing phase, as in the norming phase, it is essential that individuals bring their knowledge, influence and skills to bear on the task at hand. Cooperative behaviour now needs to take precedence over competitive behaviour.

Tendencies toward judgemental, punitive or other destructive behaviour needs to be curbed and transformed into constructive suggestion. The key principle here is the harmonizing of contributions to the group.

In the mourning phase the tasks for the individual are celebration and closure, finishing off the job, and saying goodbye.

LEADING AND FOLLOWING

You will need to have a general sense of how to participate across the developmental stages of the group and have some idea how you are going to manage issues of inclusion, control and affection (see pp. 148–149). In addition, there is a range of specific skills which will help you as a participant in most groups.

Classically, participants in groups will tend to wait until the leader initiates action, gives permission or generally gets things going. In many cases participants are conformist, compliant and even subservient to a significant degree. This may be useful behaviour in some of the security or armed forces, but it is of little value in most other sorts of groups.

It is increasingly becoming clear that leadership is simply a function which can and needs to be carried out by other people besides the designated or responsible leader. Many successful leaders now encourage all members to become 'effective' leaders, that is, capable of performing the leadership function.

What this means in practice is that all participants need to develop their influencing skills to a high degree. They need to bring this to bear on the group activities, even though they may not be the official leader.

Remember that every time you influence what goes on in the group you are effectively leading the group. Every time you are influenced by others you are effectively following their leadership.

As a group participant you can be proactive (initiating action) rather than reactive. In general the greater and the more effective your input the more satisfying the outcome, though you will probably have experienced notable exceptions.

THE ENERGY CYCLE

Nurturing

Energizing

Action

Relaxing

If a group is going to function effectively it is essential that members not only participate but do so in a way which is in harmony with, or complements, participation of other group members. In many groups some people are planning, others are going into action, and some are evaluating what is going on simultaneously. This may result in considerable frustration, possibly resentment, and probably ineffective or inefficient group performance.

Where the whole group is needed to complete a task it will help greatly if participants are aware of the need to coordinate and harmonize the way in which they carry it out. One way of getting group members to harmonize is to help them be aware of the natural energy cycle which can be used to guide people's behaviour.

The four stages of the cycle include:

● Nurturing, when people help, support, include and share information.
● Energizing, in which participants propose, initiate, decide, push their ideas, build excitement, challenge and confront.
● Performing, when members move into action, channel their energy into tasks and reach a satisfying peak or climax when action is complete.
● Relaxing, in which the participants celebrate, tie up loose ends, show and accept appreciation, reflect on and enjoy their achievement.

This cycle reflects the natural rise and fall of energy in your body as you move from rest into action and back again. There will always be high and low energy points in a group. But the group will be more satisfying and successful if participants are aware of these energy phases and use them to integrate and unify their efforts with those of the group.

★ TRY THIS NOW!

The following questions may help you to be more proactive in dealing with interpersonal problems in groups.
● *What keeps happening over and over again that leaves someone feeling bad?*
● *How does it start?*
● *What happens next?*
● *How does each person feel when it ends?*
● *How could you/they do it differently?*
Identify problem interactions which you have in groups and answer these questions in relation to specific incidents.

★ REMEMBER!

For effective participation in groups:
● *Clarify the group goals and decide your level of commitment to them.*
● *Sort out the steps that need to be taken for the group to reach its goal.*
● *Work out the group processes that will be used, for example, decision making, planning, conflict resolution or monitoring.*
● *Clarify your role and make sure others know about it and agree to it.*
● *Identify how the group will recognize effective participation.*
● *Quantify how the group will measure its progress.*

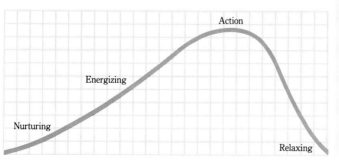

There are a number of ways in which a group can be influenced. These, outlined by British consultant John Heron, apply to most groups. They are presented as so-called polarities, pairs of opposites which are of equal value. Their appropriateness is evaluated in relation to the particular context in which they are applied, and to the goals and the belief system of the influencer. In practice, a group and its members will need to move between the extremes of each polarity in various group situations.

DIRECTIVE AND NONDIRECTIVE

This set of skills is mainly concerned with the use of power in groups. The range of options is from autocratic or unilateral decisions and action to the absence of any type of direction.

In practice this could mean that you order, request, correct, evaluate, suggest or recommend if you wish to be more directive.

Usually groups need a more democratic style of direction. People tend to be more committed to decision making when they have been consulted, or when they have made decisions that will affect them personally. The use of proposing, negotiating and other aspects of joint decision making result in power sharing.

INTERPRETIVE AND NONINTERPRETIVE

This polarity is concerned with the generation of information and meaning. Skills here range from straightforward telling to withholding information in situations where it would be appropriate to do so.

Sometimes the group will require information about why it should do something, for example a rationale or theory input. At other times it may require interpretation of some new data, an analysis of a problem, or need to formulate the implications of a particular course of action.

The most common skill used within this polarity is that of feedback. Sharing observation, opinions, interpretations and feelings will help group members learn more about themselves and improve the way they perform tasks. Being noninterpretive often means getting the group to interpret for themselves.

CONFRONTING AND NONCONFRONTING

The level of challenge in the group, and the way it is handled, are central to group functioning. Too much challenge will result in lowering of morale, confidence and safety. Too little will result in boredom and lack of interest.

Equally the manner in which the challenge or confrontation is made will often determine its success. The trick here is to confront a behaviour, an attitude or lack of knowledge while supporting the group as a whole.

If you need to confront be brief and to the point, but only after the group has agreed to receive your challenge. Let it go before you get into an argument. Remember confrontation, by its very nature, always results in some discomfort or shock for participants.

Confronting skills include getting appropriately angry, unmasking dishonest behaviour, giving confronting feedback and pointing out inconsistency in thinking (see pp. 130–131).

Nonconfronting skills include backing off, interrupting and building trust and safety in the group by introducing nonchallenging fun activities to the group.

CATHARTIC AND NONCATHARTIC

This polarity is concerned with the conscious release of tension and pent up feeling in a group. People bring tensions to a group, but over the period of time most groups inevitably experience a build up of tension and feelings. The group needs to find a way of releasing these feelings nondestructively (cathartic) or being able to move away from them (noncathartic).

Cathartic techniques include games, psychodrama and bioenergetic exercises. Cathartic techniques can enable groups to re-energize and free up the ways in which members relate to each other. When levels of distress are comparatively minor, group members achieve release through laughter, stretching and yawning.

Noncathartic techniques include meditation, a switch of activity, or switching of the attention to less distressing issues. Or people may engage in thinking, reflecting and logical activities.

STRUCTURING AND NONSTRUCTURING

This polarity is concerned with how the group is enabled to carry out its activities. Structuring involves predetermining roles, steps, sequences, processes and time to a high degree. By nonstructuring a group can allow an appropriate structure – or no definite structure – to emerge.

Typical forms of structuring include the formation of rules and guidelines, and definition of roles, geographical location and contracts. Further methods may be used to structure the way people interact, for example, through subgrouping, problem solving, planning processes and strategies for conflict resolution.

High levels of structuring tend to increase safety, low levels tend to raise the level of anxiety. Structures need to be reviewed often to check whether they are enhancing or inhibiting group performance.

Nonstructuring includes being a model member or even being absent from the group.

DISCLOSING AND NONDISCLOSING

You disclose yourself all the time in both verbal and nonverbal ways, for example, through your observations, opinions, knowledge, and eye contact, voice, posture, gesture and choice of clothes. What you do and how you do it are usually more influential than the content of what you say. When you disclose yourself appropriately, and focus all your attention on the here and now, you are said to have presence. This presence also relates to being supportive in a group.

How together you are (that is, the congruence of word and deed, verbal and nonverbal messages) comes across as you relate to others. This gives them some sense of your integrity, credibility and consistency. The greater the coherence, and the more you can be fully present to and for the group, the more you are likely to influence it.

Appropriate disclosure of experience in relation to a group task or process is likely to be supportive. At other times attentive silence, or being nondisclosing and creating space for others can be your most effective contribution.

★ TRY THIS NOW!

Take each of these polarities in turn and assess your behaviour in groups relative to them.

● *Where are your strengths and what are the skills you might usefully develop to extend your range?*

● *Identify specific new ways of influencing groups, or identify skills you could use. It will take time, so*

develop one or two skills at a time. Do not forget to get feedback on how successful you are.

Many of the titles included in the following list have been used in the writing of this book. The list is also intended as a recommendation for further reading.

MAPPING YOUR LIFE

Pierro Ferrucci
What We May Be
Turnstone Press, 1984

Carl Jung
Modern Man In Search Of A Soul
Routledge & Kegan Paul, 1961

Carl Jung
The Undiscovered Self
Mentor, 1957

Ira Progoff
The Symbolic And The Real
Coventure, 1963

M. Smith
A Practical Guide To Value Clarification
University Associates, 1980

John O. Stevens
Awareness
Real People Press, 1971

Francis Wickes
The Inner World Of Choice
Covernture, 1977

Mike Woodcock and Dave Francis
The Unblocked Manager
Gower, 1982

SELF-ESTEEM

Barbara Sher
Wishcraft
Ballantine, 1979

Alice Miller
The Drama Of The Gifted Child
Faber, 1983

Abraham Maslow
Motivation and Personality
Harper and Row, 1954

Virginia Satir
People Making
Souvenir Press, 1978

Virginia Satir
Self-Esteem And Making Contact
Souvenir Press, 1978

Marjorie Shaevitz
The Superwoman Syndrome
Fontana, 1985

MANAGING YOUR CAREER

Klaus Bochan and Jenny Lees Spalding
The Alternative Careers Book
PaperMac, 1988

Richard Bolles
What Colour Is Your Parachute
Ten Speed Press, 1981

Dave Francis
Managing Your Career
Fontana, 1985

Dave Francis and Mike Woodcock
Fifty Activities For Self Development
Gower, 1982

Ronnie Lessem
The Roots Of Excellence
Fontana, 1986

DEVELOPING YOUR CAPABILITIES

Roberto Assaglio
Psychosynthesis
Turnstone Press, 1975

Roberto Assaglio
Act Of Will
Turnstone Press, 1974

Edward De Bono
Practical Thinking
Pelican, 1976

Edward De Bono
Six Thinking Hats
Pelican, 1988

Tony Buzan
Use Your Head
BBC, 1974

Eugene Gendlin
Focusing
Bantam Press, 1981

Jean Housten
The Possible Human
J.P. Tarcher Inc., 1982

Jean Housten and Robert Masters
Mind Games
Delta, 1970

Jean Housten and Robert Masters
Listening To Your Body
Delta, 1979

Alexander Lowen, MD and Leslie Lowen
The Way To Vibrant Health
Harper Colophon, 1977

Colin Rose
Accelerated Learning
Topaz Publishing, 1985

Frances Vaughan
Awakening Intuition
Anchor Books, 1979

MANAGING YOURSELF EFFECTIVELY

Tom Boydell and Mike Pedler
Managing Yourself
Fontana, 1985

Tom Boydell, Mike Pedler and John Burgoyne
A Manager's Guide To Self Development
McGraw Hill, 1986

Alan Lakein
*How To Get Control Of Your Time
And Your Life*
Signet, 1983

Gail Sheehy
Passages
Bantam, 1977

Arthur Young
The Manager's Handbook
Sphere Books, 1986

MANAGING STRESS

Meg Bond and James Kilty
Practical Methods Of Dealing With Stress
HPRP Surrey University, 1982

L. Chaitow
Relaxation And Meditation Techniques
Thorsons, 1983

Anne Dickson
A Woman In Your Own Right
Quartet Books, 1982

Rose Evison and Richard Horobin
How To Change Yourself And The World
Co-Counselling Phoenix, Sheffield, 1983

Alexander Lowen
Biogenergetics
Penguin, 1976

Jane Madders
Stress And Relaxation
Martin Dunitz, 1979

Christina Maslach
Burn Out The Cost Of Caring
Prentice Hall, 1982

COMMUNICATION

R. Alberti and M. Emmons
Your Perfect Right
Impact Books, 1986

Michael Argyle
Bodily Communication
Methuen, 1975

Eric Berne
Games People Play
Penguin, 1964

Robert Carkhuff
The Art Of Helping
Human Resource Development Press, 1980

Gerard Egan
*You And Me – The Skills Of Communicating
And Relating To Others*
Brooks Cole, 1977

Milo O Frank
*How To Get Your Point Across In Thirty
Seconds Or Less*
Corgi Books, 1987

Liz Greene
Relating
Coventure, 1977

Muriel James and Dorothy Jongeward
Born To Win
Addison-Wesley, 1971

GETTING THINGS DONE

Ken and Kate Bach
Assertiveness At Work
McGraw Hill, 1982

Robert Bolton
People Skills
Prentice Hall, 1978

Ronnie Eisenberg and Piato Kelly
Organise Yourself
Piatkus, 1988

Dave Francis and Don Young
Improving Work Groups
University Associates, 1979

Peter Honey
Improve Your People Skills
I.P.M., 1988

Max Taylor
Coverdale On Management
Heinemann, 1979

DEALING WITH DIFFICULT PEOPLE

R. Alberti and M. Emmons
Your Perfect Right
Impact Books, 1986

Thomas Harris
I'm Okay You're Okay
Pan Books, 1973

Virginia Satir
People Making
Souvenir Press, 1972

SUPPORT SYSTEMS

J.A. Adams
Understanding And Managing Stress
University Associates, San Diego, 1980

Sheila Ernst and Lucy Goodison
In Our Own Hands
Womens Press, 1981

Barrie Hopson and Mike Scally
Build Your Own Rainbow
Life Skills Associates, 1984

James Kilty
Self And Peer Assessment
HPRP Surrey University, 1978

Stuart Miller
Men And Friendship
Gateway Books, 1983

BEING A GROUP MEMBER

Eric Berne
The Structure And Dynamics Of Organisations And Groups
Ballantine Books, 1963

Tom Douglas
Groups
Tavistock, 1983

Gaie Houston
The Red Book Of Groups
Rochester Foundation, London, 1984

D.W. Johnson and F. Johnson
Joining Together
Prentice Hall, 1975

Michael Locke
How To Run Committees And Meetings
MacMillan, 1980

Robyn Skynner and John Cleese
Families
Methuen, 1983

The following addresses include resources for both assistance and information. Their relevance to personal management is explained briefly.

CAREER DEVELOPMENT

ASSESSMENT AND GUIDANCE
6A Bedford Street
London WC1
Self-inventory and aptitude interviews.

CAREER ANALYSTS
Career House
90 Gloucester Place
London W1H 4BL
Self-inventory and career interviews.

MLM CONSULTANTS
High Leybourne Lodge
Hascombe, Surrey GU8 4AD
Management development, life/career planning, interpersonal skills training.

CAREER GUIDANCE CONSULTANTS
Hootton Lawn
Benty Health Lane
Hootton, Wirral, Cheshire WL66 6AG
General careers information.

THE CAREERS AND OCCUPATIONAL INFORMATION CENTRE
Room W1101
Training Commission
Moorfoot
Sheffield SH1 4PQ
General careers information.

CENTRE FOR PROFESSIONAL AND EXECUTIVE CAREER DEVELOPMENT AND COUNSELLING (CEPEC)
Sundrige Park Management Centre
Bromley, Kent
Careers guidance service specializing in early retirement and redundancy.

NATIONAL ADVISORY CENTRE ON CAREERS FOR WOMEN
Drayton House
Gordon Street
London WC1
Careers guidance service specializing in women returning to work.

PAULINE HIDE AND ASSOCIATES LIMITED
20 Lincolns Inn Fields
London WC2A 3ED
Outplacement consultants, career transition programmes for senior executives and re-employment programmes.

VOCATIONAL GUIDANCE CENTRE
35 Corn Exchange Building
Manchester M4
Basic careers and vocational guidance.

PERSONAL DEVELOPMENT AND COMMUNICATION SKILLS

C.A.E.R.
Rosemerryn, Lamorna
Penzance, Cornwall
Centre for self-development, with transpersonal approaches.

CENTRE FOR TRANSPERSONAL PSYCHOLOGY
7 Pembridge Place
London W2 4XB
Transpersonal approaches to self-development.

THE COVERDALE ORGANISATION LTD
Dorland House
14–16 Regent Street
London SW1Y 4PH
Organisation development, training, team building, etc.

FARQUAHAR
Consultancy Services
10 Cranbourne Avenue
Wanstead, London E11 2BQ
Self-development, coaching, and stress management policies for organizations and individuals.

THE GESTALT CENTRE
66 Warwick Road
St Albans, Hertfordshire AL1 4DL
Gestalt approaches to self-development.

HUMAN POTENTIAL RESOURCE GROUP
Department of Education Studies
University of Surrey
Guildford, Surrey GU2 5HX

LIFESKILLS
Clarendon Chambers
51 Clarendon Road
Leeds LS2 9NZ
Distance learning materials for self-development.

METANOIA
11 Tring Avenue
London W5 3QA
Gestalt and transactional analysis approaches to team and self-development.

OPENINGS
Bluecoat House
Sawclose, Bath BA1 1EY
Various courses on self-development and psychotherapy.

PRAXIS
132 Weston Park
London N8 9PN
Consultancy applying principles and practice
of humanistic psychology to industry,
education and the arts.

REDWOOD WOMEN'S TRAINING
ASSOCIATION
Invergarry
Kitilings Lane
Walton on Hill
Stafford ST17 0LE
Courses on assertiveness, sexuality, self-
esteem, etc. for women.

THE SELF-MANAGEMENT PROGRAMME
Brunel University
Uxbridge, Middlesex UB8 3PH
Varied courses on self-development and self-
management.

HEALTH AND RELAXATION

DEVONSHIRE CLINIC
21 Devonshire Place
London W1N 1PD
Holistic health care clinic specializing in
executive stress.

CENTRE FOR AUTOGENIC TRAINING
101 Harley Street
London W1
Courses and individual work in self-generated
modes of stress reduction.

THE ISIS CENTRE
362 High Road
Tottenham, London N17
Humanistic approaches to self-development
and health care.

RELAXATION FOR LIVING
Dunesk
29 Burwood Park Road
Walton on Thames, Surrey KT12 5LH

THE WORLD OF YOGA
Acacia House
Centre Avenue
Acton Vale, London W3 7JX

YOGA FOR HEALTH FOUNDATION
Ickwell Bury
Northill, Nr. Biggleswade
Bedfordshire